Robert has been working with Tech and Digita[illegible] just that and built his first website using the HTML For Dummies book in 1996. Having learned how to build websites using Google's search engine, he later moved to Switzerland and worked with EF Education and a bunch of other tech companies until today where he is an active CTO for a bunch of startups. Robert lives in Engelberg with his youngest son and most beautiful wife, with their wildest dog.

The Mejlerö Company GmbH
Blumenweg 12
6390 Engelberg
Switzerland
mejlero.com

The CTO Playbook is a book for people who are working with developers in tech teams. Here you are going to get insights which can be useful when hiring, building products, choosing technology, leading and communicating. Topics are divided into chapters about

People, Work, Tech, Leadership and Communication.

INTRO

The art of developing an application has been well described in various coding books that you can find gathering dust on almost all developers desks around the world. This is not that book. There may be some technical references, but astonishing few of them considering this is a CTO-book. And why's that? This is a book for people who ended up in the situation of having to work with other people building applications — also known as "developers". Fresh CTO's, Product People or whoever is interested in leading dev teams can also benefit from reading this book. Spoiler alert: you will not learn to code here, nor do I have all the answers to everything. However I've put together my thoughts and experience based on working for various companies in various industries. Or, more importantly, working with different groups of people in different settings, getting an application together from scratch. So that's what this book is about. Yep, there will be a few pointers and ideas. No, I'm not claiming to know it all. But you've read this far and now thinking if you want to continue to check out the rest, so why not? I've put together some topics where I think I could contribute. Happy reading!

CHAPTER 0

THE JOURNEY

Here is a quick outline of the different topics you will find in this book. We can call it the journey map of the book.

Nothing will be done without great **people**. We start the journey by visiting this important topic. Hiring, setting fair salaries and make a proper onboarding helps you set the basics. If it's not going like intended, we also need to talk about firing and off-boarding.

With the right people on board, we want to start building great things. There are a lot to think about here, in order to not waste time and resources. Setting the right business priorities are crucial for the success of the project or the product. Streamlining how we **work** and how we get from idea to done is also covered.

Get your nerdy glasses on for the **tech** chapters, giving people new to tech a great lingo start, and a refresher for the seasoned. We talk about coding in general, frontend, backend differences as well as devops. We touch maintenance, documentation and how to handle incidents.

Working with technology and developers may be different from finance, but the same **leadership** principles applies here too, with a little twist. Leadership in tech, avoiding micro management, motivation and feedback are other topics touched.

Presenting, packaging information and manage budgets lives under **communication**. Here you can also find the Forbidden Words List which can help moving from older concepts to new, fresh and modern thinking.

With the distinction of the chapters you will have a clear journey, even though many of the chapters can be read individually and may not be completely connected.

PEOPLE – **who**

WORK – **how**

TECH – **what**

LEADERSHIP – **support**

COMMUNICATION – **talk**

5 important ingredients for you who are working with tech projects.

Now it's time to begin your journey thru the book!

PEOPLE

The single most important thing in order to be able to work with development of new great products – is to get the right people on board. It's much more important that people with the right attitude, ambition, willingness to cooperate and drive joins, than if they have the right education. Great people doesn't grow on trees. They sit behind computers all around the world waiting to join your great company. Now you just have to find **who**.

CHAPTER 1

HIRING THE RIGHT PEOPLE

Getting the right people on board is as hard as it sounds.

Having the right people on the team is of course very important. But who are the right people and where can you find them? Not so easy. Finding your future coworkers takes a lot of time and effort, and as in other parts on this playbook we are not able to cover the steps in detail.

For me it all starts with understanding what you need for your project (later product). Do you “just” need a developer who can get the application idea out fast or do you need long term co-workers who thinks and acts in the best interest of the company and your vision? Big difference. Now, to just hire a developer to “fix things” is not really a good solution. You will most likely need an entire team of developers who continuously builds features and "fixes things” so we'll focus in the latter case — getting someone great onboard your team. Does the same principle apply to developers as with other staff? Yes, they do.

Now, you are itching to just put out that add on LinkedIn and start interviewing people, and that is really not as bad of an approach as it sounds. During this process you'll meet different kinds of people and hear about different skills. You will learn a lot. However you are taking up the time of someone else your are not paying (yet) so the fully agile/ test approach may not be ethically ok here to be honest. My experience is that it's better to be clear when hiring, but at the same time be able to adjust if someone shows other skills you didn't think of. Avoiding to stuff the job ad full with buzz words is of course another thing to avoid.

I have hired "others" than developers but I'll leave those specifics out. When I hire developers I try to of course understand the need, and then do a mix of advertisement and direct contact (aka head hunting).

If you have low budget I would suggest an approach of doing it yourself or via LinkedIn. Some companies have HR Business Partners who can short list and get great lists of candidates, but many small companies can't do that. You could also consider outsourcing development. This is a big topic. Remember that if you do that, technical knowledge of your product will land with an external vendor, so stick to common development frameworks and processes and "best practice" architecture that comes from some frameworks, rather than re-inventing wheels. Also it's easier for another outsourcing company to pick up where someone left.

Always keep a clause in the contract for handover (aka Knowledge Transfer) so you're not stuck to a vendor.

Now back to hiring to your "internal team". Put together a job ad which you run by a developer or "tech person" so that there's no weird stuff in there such as "15 years of experience from X technology" if it didn't even exist 15 years ago.

Remember that everyone else also offers free coffee, ping pong table and a cool office. Consider offering flexible working hours, generous free time off, remote work and if possible even flexible working location, such as in other countries. Could be tricky with tax but you will tap in to a much bigger talent pool this way.

Now that you have your ad, you still need to get developers to apply, which is not that easy. Share it in your network and consider sharing and put your ad on other platforms where developers hangs out like Stack Overflow, local job board websites or similar. You will also be contacted by recruiters who offers their services for up to 23% of the first annual salary. Is it worth it? Could be. Depends. But it quickly gets expensive.

If you have a reputation as a good employer, a strong name or interesting products that developers wants to work with, you are of course going to be more successful.

A note here is that developers are a picky bunch of people who knows they can get a job almost anywhere as their guild is in great demand. Hence many developers seek "a place where I can finally tolerate to work" or where they can work and learn new technologies.

It's also my experience that it is much better to hire someone who is not very senior and strong minded about certain solutions, but someone who's open to learn. Developers are quick learners by nature so don't get blinded by the job spec. At the same time a balance. If you are building something complex, you could also save a lot of time finding the right person with the right skill rather than having someone going thru a learning process to get there.

Remember that a hiring process is not only about interviewing developers and see if they are a good fit for your job, but as much the candidates chance to get to know you, your company and the culture you have. It's a two-way street.

Letting the potential candidates talk to co-workers could be a good idea as it would help them in their process of selecting their next employer.

A typical hiring process

Make a profile
Write down which skills you are looking for and make a job profile that clearly describes the role. This is the base for the job advertisement that you are putting out in the job boards. Developers applying for your job will read this in detail, so be clear to mention which tech stack you are

working with. (Wow, new word? Tech Stack? Read more about Programming Languages). Putting salaries in job descriptions? Depends. It could be fair to put a range, but you on one hand don't want exaggerated expectations, and on the other hand don't want to have to junior applicants with less experience. Many companies choose to not set the salary range in the job ad, and instead discuss it in the interview. I think that's fair, as long as the company then is ready to be "off budget" with many candidates later when deciding.

Culture
Write a section about the company culture and don't make the text too "corporate". Do you really have a flat hierarchy and can anyone talk to anyone without any red tape? Again, developers chose you too.

Match applicants with the job specifics
Once applications comes in, try "look beyond the CV". Of course, some basics will have to be met, but checking the developers Stack Overflow profiles, their GitHub accounts (where they have code examples) could be much more useful than just blindly looking at resumes. This is a long process and some online tools can help. Asking developers early of their salary expectation is a good way to see if you are on budget. Asking when they can start is a good way to see if you have the right timing.

Conduct interviews
The next natural step is to talk to the candidates in an online meeting. What to ask? It's notoriously hard to get *some*

developers to talk about motivation, their 5-year plan or anything else really than just coding. If you are a communicative human being, you may seek to "click" and "get inspired" in an interview. Make sure you direct these efforts towards understanding the skill of the developer instead, as they have absolutely nothing to do with how good the developer is or not. Some of the best developers I've worked with didn't say too much during the interviews, rather than answering questions. So be prepared. At the same time, some developers can talk intensively about coding practices, why they chose a special programming language or be very talkative when asked to explain a certain topic. If the developer is going to be in a position where they need to communicate a lot with other people on the company, you may feel that it's important that they can express themselves on a not "weird way". If this is really important or not depends how you are going to work with the developers. Are you stuffing them in to your office or are you mainly going to communicate via Teams or Slack, mostly in writing?

Selection
Choosing who to work with is a mix of budget, the by you experienced attitude of the candidate, observed or reported skills and timing. And a match is a match. And if there's a match.

Offering
Once you have decided who, you need to get the candidate a great offer. That doesn't only mean salary, it also means working conditions like remote work, vacation, flexible

working hours, to mention a few. If you had a budget about a certain salary range, it doesn't make sense to offer anything less than the salary expectation of the developer. Best case the developer declines. Worst case they accept and join your company, only to be demotivated very quick and may seek other jobs instead of engaging with your company. If you have a great candidate which is a great match, it's maybe a good idea to try to get a higher budget instead and to offer them what they want. They will be motivated. On the other hand, if they come back with counter-offers and are asking for much more than what you are comfortable to offer, it's better to not force it. Read more in the next chapter What to pay.

Closing

It's only fair to inform the other applicants that they are not being considered. The worst thing for developers (and everyone else for that matter) is when recruiters or hiring managers never get back. It's a sign of respect, no matter if you have 1000 applications or 5.

CHAPTER 2

WHAT TO PAY

What is the time from someones life worth?

The topic of salaries and renumeration is a huge topic that deserves its own book. My take on it is that people should be paid fairly, to their market "value" and "enough".

Up to a certain level, getting a salary is needed for survival. The employee needs to buy food, have shelter and warmth. Leaving Maslow's Theory of Needs (1943) right here, we are talking about what happens after that level is met; after all we are all in "self-actualisation", the lucky top of the triangle in the world that can even have the luxury to think about this.

■■

Motivation can be both intrinsic and extrinsic. Once we have the "Hygiene factors" met such as people have an ok computer to work with, somewhere to sit and work, colleagues or some other factors met — the topic of salary is a big topic. If you pay much more than everyone else, you are of course appreciating your staff and in a way sharing profit fair, but it could also attract employees that's only in it for the money; they are extrinsically motivated. They will, paradoxically, work less for more pay. Their main motivation is to make money. I don't know about you, but I would like to work with people who's main motivation is to build great products. Of course everyone wants more money, so be fair and increase the salary in parity with profits and gradually every year instead of the employees having to ask for it. Otherwise the discussion will be around salary all the time.

With this said, it's absolutely crucial that people are hired in the right way, local taxes are paid, they are insured and that they can take sick leave and other time off when they need without being in financial limbo. This is even more important when working with consultants from third party vendors in India, Vietnam or elsewhere. It's a trap to just pay with Paypal. It's not good to put the employee/consultant in that kind of situation.

If you don't pay to the salary expectations, they will leave. Not directly, but after a while. And, they'll go thru tons of interviews and spend energy thinking about their future, while working for you, instead of coding. So in a way it's self-adjusting. It just seems that some never learns. Some companies also engage in the bidding-game trying to pay less than what the employees salary expectation is. That's a route to disaster. The hiring market of today are super liquid and almost any developer can pick and choose from where they want to work, and offers are raining in from startups, innovations hubs, corporates and everyone else in need of developers. Better to be fair here, and use the allocated budget, than to save a few 1000 a year which really works the opposite way.

When it comes to bonus, I always see it as, wait for it – a *bonus*. It should be paid out when the company made some great profit or got a certain deal and employees were extra out of the ordinary in making it happen. If people starts to expect it – it works against its purpose. This also means that I think it's unfair to set high variable bonus goals for developers. If you work "harder" or "faster" as a developer, which usually means putting in more hours, to complete a certain feature – are you then contributing to the bottom line of the company enough to justify a variable pay? It's a slippery slope. With Kanban and similar development processes it's better to keep a steady pace than to rush.

You can keep beers and other drinks free. It doesn't cost much. But is it really a big perk worth mentioning? Perhaps then only for those working in an office, which is not so many anymore. Maybe find something else that can benefit everyone. Free local gym card? Always two hours off during lunch for whatever free activity away from the computer? Free training courses? I'm just shooting from the hip here but I'm fairly sure that free drinks is not going to be why someone chooses to work with your company.

CHAPTER 3

ONBOARDING

Getting new developers up to speed and give them a warm welcome.

One thing is for sure. You will be doing this activity together with new people joining your company many times. No matter how much don't want people to leave and you are told "ensure that everyone stays!" by some delusional CEO, people do indeed come and go. So it's a great idea to have a process for it. Also, it'll help you handle new excited joiners in their first days of the company, when they are still curious and non-indoctrinated. And what's better for motivation than getting a warm welcome?

Working with onboarding lists helps you keep the onboarding organised, tracked and visual. Putting clear actors to each activity that needs to be happening ensures a clear ownership and nothing will fall thru the cracks. On top of the onboarding list for developers should of course be to get them access to all the needed systems and get them a good new computer so they can get started right away.

Introduction plans with other devs, demos of code and functionality, going thru dev processes etc is also great to have, but it would from my point of view be even nicer to arrange 1:1 meetings with everyone in the team so they could meet and greet and get to know. We always worked with buddy systems so that a person is responsible for helping and getting them up to speed.

Setting up invitations with the other departments is also a good idea. No, you don't need Powerpoint slides, long preparations or even agendas. You need a coffee or whatever you drink, and a get to know meeting. People will not be critical to the business (normally) in the first week. They'll can talk about easy stuff like the weather, hobbies and favourite foods. They'll try to find common denominators with others and see how the other person reacts to their communication. You don't need to be there. People are adults. If you instead of the above, try to be "efficient" and "sausage stuff" your meetings with tons of information, org charts, roles, names of employees and their responsibilities etc, it's a good chance that if not all, then at least 95%, is forgotten. Then the new employee will not dare to ask again and some good info was lost. My experience is that waiting with all that until it's needed is the better move.

The entire purpose of the onboarding is to give the new employee a great start and feel welcome but also to expand their internal network and know who they can talk to about what.

A great exercise when a new person joins is to have them write down their experience, their understanding of the company's offering and check the website. With these fresh eyes you can get a lot of great insights in to things that was not visible to you, because you worked with it so long you got blind. Getting this feedback is also a great way to show the new employee you are listening to inputs.

CHAPTER 4

OUTSOURCING

You want in-house developers sitting next to you?

If you look at job ads for developers, they are "usually" pretty much alike. There is an intro about what the company do, then some role info and some perks. Most also states that there is an office space that should be visited every day (so called "onsite"). Some has moved to the incredible land of "Hybrid". If you hire developers to work in an office they would need to use headphones in order to be able to work in the open office space.

Now, many companies has stopped working like that. Many companies offers remote work, because of the main reason (a part from what they spin) is that they couldn't find any developers who wanted to work for them otherwise. Yes, that's how remote work really started, long time before Covid-19.

■■

There is a huge scarcity of developers all around the world, but mainly in the countries which has the companies based that needs them the most. I don't mean the consultancy companies, but the Product companies. It's extremely hard to find talent locally, not that it doesn't exist, but because they already have jobs — with a pretty good pay. So the only way to get them to work for you would be to pay them more and offer better conditions. Most developers are "habit animals" and don't really like to move around. We are all different of course. One developer once said: "finally I found someone I can tolerate to work with". Funny. Point is — it's going to be expensive and time consuming. Again if you are a known brand with a name like Spotify (even though I know even they have to recruit internationally and relocate — they took a very good developer from Maersk Digital in Denmark when I worked as an Agile coach there), or Klarna - you could perhaps use your fame and coolness but even these companies offer remote work to attract global talent.

Why is this relevant to outsourcing? Because outsourcing was and is an alternative to setup your own team. You go out and find a partner who can do it for you instead. In some cases you don't even need to be involved. You can just create your Requirements specification, your Functional Specification of your product and approach a few development partners. You still need to be involved. If you choose the classic waterfall project track (where you specify what you are going to do before you do it and engage in a phased project approach with testing in the end, versus the agile approach where you work in small iterations instead to have something potentially ready to be released all the time) — you still get the same issues as everyone else. Maybe even worse as you may have based your contract on the first thoughts and ideas you had about the requirements, which most likely changed during the development process as you learned more and more — and hence the incentive and drive from your outsourcing partner is to deliver exactly what that requirements document said because then they get paid. Any change costs extra and any incentive of continuous improvement is thus gone.

You can outsource to an Agile partner who will work more closely with you to work of your Backlog or planned sprints, and this could be a good and cost effective way to hiring your own team. Working with agile contracts is still very new and requires the buyer (you) to be very active and continuously test and improve by giving feedback.

Near-shoring is another concept when you may find partners near you like in Ukraine (before Russia invaded Ukraine there were tons of great companies working with Product Development there. Many had to leave their jobs to go to war. Still many are active and are great developers.), Portugal or Poland. The near-shoring concept came about because of lower salaries but also because it's the same time zone and similar culture. Also it's not too far away when you want to travel and meet in person.

Many of these setups may pose a problem as you don't really know who's working on your code, unless you know the developers by name. Sometimes you could work with many different developers that are shared on many other projects or "cycled" around. You could get junior developers being trained on your own code base and you may not be in a position or have the experience and skills to inspect their code. This could lead to a "black box" situation where it's hard to judge the quality and you are always "in the lap" of your partner. They know and control all the code and you have to go to them (and their price list) to make any changes. It's not the best situation to end up in, as you just wanted to build your own application, but got all these complexities.

When I was working with EF Education in Lucerne and Zürich, we moved from working with an outsourced team in Chennai (India) to setup our own team in Bangalore. They were employed directly by EF, just like the other 30.000+ staff around the world and they were working directly with Product Managers in Europe and US. Not everything was working perfect, I think mostly because of the current management and the "us and them feeling" but overall the concept was very good and a lot of things was getting done. Now, having your own 250+ heads developers doesn't save you from building crappy systems, if you are not listening to your developers. So this brings me to the favoured option of setting up distributed teams, and manage (lead) them yourself.

Body lease, is a bad word for it and the better word would be "dedicated team". Basically you hire developers directly to be employed by your company, either thru a contracting partner that employs locally, or you setup your own entity. I would vote for using someone local, as it's a lot to do with hiring like HR, salaries, taxes, insurances as well as sick leave, vacation and more that you may now want or have time to do. The end result is the same though. You get developers that works directly with you, without any other middle men. In this way, you can work with your dedicated team just like if they were your local employees that just was working from home. You can give them the same working structure, same development processes, same working flexibility and flat organisational structure. Instead of giving your developers a specification, you could ask them how they would solve it. And magic will happen. They will instead deliver great code and be proud about it. In some cases when you are working with with Partners/ outsourcing companies in India, you usually get a set hierarchy. Project Manager, Tech lead, Senior Developer, Junior Developer and Trainee for example. This old school and outdated structure makes development inefficient. Some developers are only involved in one part of a solution and never gets to see the entire process. Also, as they don't have the "say" and the job title, they don't get listened to.

With your own dedicated team you should treat your team the same way as you treat your other developers; with respect, openness, shared responsibility and flexibility. It turns out that people who are treated well and listened to, are actually highly motivated! That's a good thing to have as you are for sure going to have other obstacles to climb over.

As you get a fixed invoice from your partner, you can easily calculate the cost of running your team. It's easy to budget, forecast and set expectations with the finance department.

Having a team in India could cost 75% less than hiring locally, but you could easily lose that margin in lost productivity if you try to manage and tell, instead of leading. So as with the rest of your team; set clear goals, use a good development process and trust your developers to deliver.

CHAPTER 5

FIRING

About bad apples and how to throw them out. That's a clickbait title for you and has nothing to do with the content of this chapter.

One person in your team is not delivering. There's a lot of subtile messaging in that sentence. Let's dig down. I think everyone in the team deserves a chance, and also an opportunity to be an individual. Because guess what, we all are. A leader that can accommodate for the very different spread of personalities, reactions, emotions, individuality, ways of expressing oneself, ways of communicating and experience situations – will be successful. Nobody said it was easy. A good leader will also see that they can not fully do all of the above, but they could try and that's already much better than most managers. The task driven managers.

Task driven managers are very focused on getting the job done (at all costs) and anyone who is not "delivering" is a bad person and is not "good". All according to the task driven manager. On the other hand you have the people-oriented leader who delegates, empowers and motivates their team(s) to find their own solutions. This is a great recipe for building autonomous self-organised teams. And, if you may, “high performing”. This is relevant, as the perception of “bad apples” or “bad people” is mostly subjective.

Getting back to that sentence “One person in your team is not delivering” — it's probably coming from a task driven manager who wants to get job done, and doesn't hesitate to jump in, roll up their sleeves and do it themselves if they have to. They also know how to do things faster, better and smarter. The only reason they didn't do it in the first place is because they are the manager, and they get others to do stuff. Right.

There are many of reasons why someone in the team may not be “delivering". First of all – did they get any help? Help and support is a good thing, and everyone needs it in various form in order to grow and get “better”. (Not necessarily via someone telling them stuff, but hey lets not write an entire Agile coaching book here).

When you are pointing a finger towards someone, three is pointing back at yourself — said someone smart. So first, help, give options, shuffle around, get others to help, work with the person. They are usually not “bad".

■■

Freebie: One way to spot a task-driven manager is to ask them to describe a former colleague that contributed the least to the work. If you get an answer in the lines of "he/she was a real idiot" – you got a match! The other, more thought thru answer you'd expect from a people-oriented leader would be "I think the person may not have been in the right place".

But sometimes it has to happen. Firing. If the person has been given all support and chances that's possible to give and they have yet failed to understand (and appreciate) that they have to walk at least half of the way themselves and make both a decision, but also a commitment – to the company, the people, the processes and the product – they may need to leave. An do something else.

Nobody said this was easy. Also, nobody said it was hard either. When these situations arise, you as a leader and a representative of the company need to raise up and take your responsibility. Loop in HR and give that notice. In the US you have the (for us in EU) weird "You are fired and I'll have security escort you out right now" and the employe gets their little box with belongings and is left on the street in the rain. Or maybe that was a movie?

Anyhow, it doesn't have to be like that. Have a talk, chat, discuss and make a good plan for both the "fired" employee and the company. After the formalities, work out communication with the employee and inform the team, keep the standards high. If you are not informing, people will just guess and will anyway find out. Also don't BS grown-ups with lies and corporate BS texts. This doesn't have to be a fail – there are ways to turn this in to something good. The person is not "bad" just because it didn't work out. Look beyond the "I wasted so much time and energy with this person" and "oh no my hiring budget is blown up" or "gah I can't wait for them to leave". Make it nice and, one more tip from the coach here — there are most likely others in the team who really liked the person and needs to go thru their own personal process of accepting this. So treat it the process with respect, take a step back and let people breathe and live.

CHAPTER 6

OFF-BOARDING

Remove access, conduct interview and close down all accounts when someone is leaving – and drink the grave beers.

Removing access to systems is important, and should be done the day after the person leaves the team. Here, it's also a good idea to change access passwords to common shared developer password systems like Bitwarden, LastPass and the like. Some super paranoid organisations also changes the database passwords. Not needed if you didn't share them or used proper user management in the first place.

However there is another part of off-boarding that usually doesn't make it to the off-boarding lists. As discussed in the firing chapter, it's a good idea to host a good bye event for the person leaving, no matter why they are leaving. People need closure, and a good framing. Some well-chosen words and a drink (or virtual over Slack) is a good idea, to keep the morale of the other people in the team. It's also a good idea to not have people just continue with work again but to perhaps take the rest of the day off if they want or slow things down. Why? Because people do get affected by changes whether we like it or not.

A nice framing also gives you, their leader, a chance to celebrate the good times and go back the memory lane and share how fun you had when that code script was not working or that new feature you built got released and appreciated. A parting gift shows the company appreciates their employees. A gift card on Amazon is enough and just shows that you as a company cares. It's easy to skip all this and just bend down the head an move on to the next thing. But in my experience we are missing out on some opportunities to motivate and show appreciation to the team.

■■

Another forgotten thing is the exit interview. Now with all pressure off, there is no need for the employee to hold back and not speak their heart in the risk they may be fired. So this is again your chance to gather important feedback from their perspective. Try it, you'd be amazed. I've learned the hard way, it's not easy to sit and listen and not reply or try to defend when harsh feedback comes. It can be unjustified, full of factual errors or based on assumptions. It may certainly not be what you want to hear, but it's the (hopefully) raw feedback from another fellow human who's also an adult and have had an experience. With you and your company.

WORK

We are now moving on to the working area. Here we're going to find out how to set the right priorities, start a project, build a product and look at the development process.

CHAPTER 7

WHAT TO FOCUS ON

Business first means business first.

Beautiful code or just working code? Maintaining code or building new features and increase sales? Adhere to the development process, continuously remove technical debt, prettifying code or keeping the stack up to date? There are many things to choose from. But what is the most important?

The answer is so easy, but so often forgotten. Business comes first.

Working in departmentalised companies, we usually work in silos. We build up our own set of priorities which we hold as the most important thing. To a developer this could be "code quality" and "code readability" or even "indent code 4 spaces" or as trivial as "stick with a standard way of CamelCasingTheCode". To a marketeer it could be do get the campaign out the door and start generating leads or impressions. To an accountant may be to get the receipts, with the right company information on them (don't forget VAT) and to a customer service agent it could be to make the customer happy — because the customer is always right (nope). Everyone has their own focus.

Whatever the priority is — we can be certain we all see things from different perspectives. That's fine. We all strive to deliver our goals, KPI's or deliverables so we can get that bonus, or feel we have done our job, or left great code, or have a good legacy, increased the conversion rate or increased sales. Whatever the reason is — one thing wins over them all. Tutti. Business. Business comes first.

■■

The single reason a company exist, is, to generate wealth to their shareholders. But, this is not an economical or financial lecture. So let's be a bit more specific. The reason why the company you work for exist is to be successful; which could mean selling more, getting more clients, get better deals and in the end earn more money. If the company is not doing that, it doesn't make any difference how much we "gold plate" and do things great. The company will not go bankrupt if it's not making money. Hence, to get back on track. Blocking an important release shouldn't be justified by some less important standard is not kept or that "the wrong name convention is used in the function" or "it's not commented correctly". If you hear this from your developers, it's time to change something. People are most likely too detailed driven. I'm not saying the above is not important, because no matter how trivial it sounds, it *is* important. But to hold off a release if there is a large sales campaign or marketing event hanging on it? Nope. Business comes first. The Chief Code Reviewer (which ideally should be your entire team, not a "Tech lead" – as you'll just invent incentive for push back – must take a step back (or forth) and *facilitate* the code review and make it happen. This works well if you are working with proactive people that drives and ensures that things happen, rather than pushing back and complaining.

Same goes if a marketing campaign must go live just before everyone signs out on Friday. The risk to introduce bugs – which could jeopardise the entire product stability – over the weekend clearly is not worth it. Business comes first. In in that case it means continuity. Business continuity. If your team is forced to release new functionality on a Friday afternoon – you can rest assure good ol' Murphy will come knocking on your door – when you are taking the first bite of the family dinner. Incident time! No one wants this – so let's avoid it.

Releasing a bug-fix on Friday? Yes! Why not? As long as it's tested and is not breaking other functionality. "Normally" (with large quote marks) a bug fix is an isolated small fix to something anyway not working in production – so it's better to get it fixed. It depends on what it is. But if it solves some form problem and you can get more leads over the weekend – why wait? Business first.

Last minute changes to images? Yes! This is content, and should ideally be handled by a CMS (Content Management System), and should not be limited by having to change the code – but if it has to – well, go for it. Content changes are harmless (until you work with french languages and use an apostrophe instead of a quote, which could break the code as it's interpreted differently if used wrongly). Business first.

There's a principle called the Pareto principle which means that roughly 80% of the consequences comes from 20% of causes. So focusing on these 20% would theoretically solve 80% of the issues. If you really can identify which 20% of the bugs that makes the most of the issues – go ahead and fix them!

The key take away is that it doesn't make sense that each department drives their own agenda. Whatever potentially has the biggest impact on sales should be prioritised. It's always a balance though because neglecting key code maintenance would slowly degrade the code which in turn could potentially make it harder to do some other improvements later.

The best way to choose what to focus on is to get together the different departments and visualise a list of things that needs to be done, and prioritise together.

CHAPTER 8

AGILE

An intro to the basics of true agile.

The word "agile" can be heard in meetings and seen in presentations. There are many misunderstandings and it would make sense to discuss these, however let's start with the agile basics.

In 2001 a group of developers got together and wrote the Agile manifesto. As this manifesto gives a very good overview of what agile is, I've decided to include it.

We value

Individuals and interactions over processes and tools

Working software over comprehensive documentation

Customer collaboration over contract negotiation

Responding to change over following a plan

"That is, while there is value in the items on the right, we value the items on the left more"
– Agile Manifesto (2001) agilemanifesto.org

The group also laid out the twelve principles of Agile Software:

We follow these principles:

Our highest priority is to satisfy the customer through early and continuous delivery of valuable software.

Welcome changing requirements, even late in development. Agile processes harness change for the customer's competitive advantage.

Deliver working software frequently, from a couple of weeks to a couple of months, with a preference to the shorter timescale.

Business people and developers must work together daily throughout the project.

Build projects around motivated individuals. Give them the environment and support they need, and trust them to get the job done.

The most efficient and effective method of conveying information to and within a development team is face-to-face conversation.

Working software is the primary measure of progress.

Agile processes promote sustainable development. The sponsors, developers, and users should be able to maintain a constant pace indefinitely.

Continuous attention to technical excellence and good design enhances agility.

Simplicity--the art of maximizing the amount of work not done--is essential.

The best architectures, requirements, and designs emerge from self-organizing teams.

At regular intervals, the team reflects on how to become more effective, then tunes and adjusts its behavior accordingly.

– Agile Manifesto (2001) agilemanifesto.org

Agile is a mindset

You can't become "agile" through changing processes and adding new tools. The entire point is to be flexible, allow change and try to solve the problem, rather than putting up obstacles or excuses to not be able to do it. It all starts with the people ("motivated individuals") who works together understanding what this is and what it's not.

Agile methodologies

There are many different ways of working in an agile way, and I'm sure you can google up content about them. For the sake of complement of this book, I'm outlining two of the methodologies which I think works the best. They are called Scrum and Kanban.

Scrum

The word "scrum" is not an abbreviation. It simply means gathering and is taken from the rugby world. They have scrums planning their next moves on the field. In it's essence, scrum is a pretty simple process. Put a fully dedicated team together. Have them write down everything that's needed to be done on a Product Backlog, which is a prioritised list of User Stories. User stories are not Requirements. User stories are like "As a user I want to have X so that I can X" and hence more open ended and discussion starters than set Requirements which are more "The image must be 100px wide". Writing things in a User story way encourages developers to find solutions rather than doing what they are told. Once the list is done, the team gets together and picks out a few "stories" they think they can get done in the next two weeks. The do this Sprint planning and put the stories on a Sprint backlog. Every day during the sprint the developers update each other on the progress by answering the three questions "what did I do since yesterday, what will I do until tomorrow and I have this problem". After two weeks there's a sprint review where the team presents or showcases a potential product increment and it gets decided by the Product Owner if it's done or needs more work in a new iteration. The team also holds a retrospective to discuss things to improve in the collaboration.

Working with scrum is great and the best thing is that you can see changes and something that can be released in just two weeks. It's also motivating for the team to be working on something they can see being done directly. This also opens up for better Product development, as you can test features on real users and see how it's received before you scale up and build more features.

Kanban

The Japanese word "Kanban" means "Visual board" and was invented by Toyota in their Just-in-Time lean manufacturing process. Since 2007 it's more known as the "Kanban method" which is what we are discovering here. A Kanban development process is all about reducing waste and optimise outcome (not output). It's a development process where all participants are working at a constant pace, which in theory can be kept indefinitely. The process covers getting ideas, making them ready for development, prioritising, picking up by developers, actual development and testing as well as release. A simplified Kanban board would have To-Do, Doing and Done stages. The entire Development Process following this methodology can be found under the Development Process chapter.

Kanban uses the same basic as scrum with the main difference that it's not using time boxed sprints. Instead you can release things whenever they are done, directly without waiting out the sprint. Kanban works great for established products and not so good for completely new projects that's needs some basics before it can get to a first release.

Agile Product Development

Product development includes more components such as user research and user testing, in order to understand and also test assumption on how a product is used. These useful insights are a part of the ideation and pre-development process in one way. In true agile style it's important that "business people and developers work together daily" and I interpret this as that the teams should be cross-functional. Then we can't really have a side process for ideation without developers. I would suggest involving developers also in the ideation and preparation of feature descriptions or user stories.

Another aspect of agile is that you can't try to build a car directly. You need to break it down and work in small improvement cycles. If you want to build a car, start building a skateboard, evolve it to a kick bike, add an engine and make it a go-cart, add roof and you have your car. During all your development time the user could use your product in some way. Compare this with if you would have done a classic project, also known as "waterfall". Then you would have nothing to show to the customers until you are completely done. You will loose valuable time and most likely you are not going to build what you thought in the beginning anyway. You will get new ideas when you see the product being built out and will want other things. Agile can "welcoming change in requirements" and that's why it's so popular and widely used in Software development as well as in other business areas.

Misunderstandings

Some of the misunderstandings about agile are around planning, people and budget. Working in an agile way is simple and hence doing more complex things or trying to achieve something very demanding will need the same time as if it was done in any other methodology. What you do is breaking down the complexity and building it up rather than trying to do everything at the same time. Around people the misunderstanding usually is that you have to have a special training or need to know some extensive processes and this is also wrong. It's a good idea to take an agile training or introduction in order to get your "aha moment" but it's not needed at all. You can tag along with the others and learn. Agile is also best with self-organised teams, so there's no need for a lot of management overhead and controlling either. Stop micro managing. Budget, a topic in itself is covered und the Budget chapter. But in short, if there's something that would make a CFO happy is a steady and predictable cost for your development team. Agile gives you that.

Be aware of fake agile

Whenever something is overly complex and tells you exactly how to do things, has too many meetings, processes or external dependencies, it's not agile or at least not following the basic principles. Scrumfall is an example of classic projects working with iterations in the middle of the Execution phase. This is not the same. Also, there are some other basics that needs to be in place in order to be successful working with agile.

Basic things to make it work

Cross functional - the team needs to have both business people and developers, user experience designers and analysts or whoever needs to be involved directly in the team.

Dedicated - the agile team members needs to be 100% dedicated. They can't work on anything else.

Co-located - it was long though that the team must sit in the same room but "face-to-face conversations" can also be held over online meetings as long as the team has basic trust and no one else is sitting together physically.

Clear roles - easy one. There's only Product Owner (who's responsible to prioritise the Backlog) and participants. A ScrumMaster can facilitate the meetings and the team can take turns doing this role.

Self-organised - The team doesn't need any managers to give them other priorities. Give them a budget and let them decide how they work. Coach them if needed.

No external dependencies - sometimes hard but the more you can have the team work on their own product without having to touch anyone else's territory - the better.

CHAPTER 9

PLANNING

Plan the Kanban product development.

We need to talk about plans. One of the biggest misunderstandings about Agile is that you can't plan. It's not true. You just can't make detailed long term plans that must be followed and be super strict.

One way to handle this is to **not** make Gantt charts or excel lists with tasks, deadlines and assignments. If you do – you will be disappointed. One of the down sides with running an Agile Kanban project is that you can't say exactly when things are going to be released and done. If you do, it will most likely take longer time as you need to hold it off, dedicate developers to work on it and have business owners standing by cheering and champion it thru. Kanban is different, in that it moves from state to state in a pace that keeps up with the processing pace as the others in the system have. If you rush you will pile up at these different stations and thus create waste. It will only take longer for it to be released.

■■

There may be certain features that you may *not want to release to your users* every day. You can still release them, using feature flags or other similar functionality. It's basically a small admin system or a code feature in which you can activate features for a selected group or specific customers when you need to. This is how you make Product Owners **and** Kanban evangelists happy at the same time. It may sound crazy that you would have unused features sitting idle in the main code branch and thus released to production, however as long as they are properly managed and actively worked on, as in promoted and communicated by the Product Owner, it's ok. Otherwise it's even more waste.

In the Starting a project and Development process chapters I'm discussing using a Road map to set expectations with all parts of the organisation and you could also have (separate) ones for your customers and users. These sets the right expectations and the Product team can plan their work. It's a great idea to encourage everyone to actively discuss and bring up important upcoming development needs to your attention and make sure they are moved in and visualised on the Road Map. Now you are doing agile planning. Amazing!

Dealing with some, er...people with different perspectives may have you still needing to answer questions like "When is it ready?" and "Can I see the requirements?". Yes, none of these are parts of Agile Product Development but just because your stakeholders or peers doesn't have your great vocabulary, it doesn't mean that you can't still respond in the agile way. Show them the backlog, give high level estimates, show some notes. More about this can be found in the Project update chapter.

When I worked as an Agile coach at Maersk Digital in Copenhagen, Denmark – we had a list of "forbidden words". Milestone, deadline, resource, critical path, update meeting, approval, sign of, demo, review, audit, change request, defect – are just some examples of words that means something that goes against the agile principles. Changing a mindset also means changing the language to one extent. But we don't have to be so stiff. Today, I have no problem calling the User stories "requirements". Fine. Better to play along. Business first.

What will it cost? Instead of randomly choose to work on a project for 6 months, here you can work in iterations and talk about what you think you and your time may have achieved in 6 months instead. What you think you want to build now are most likely *not* what you actually are building later, after your first contact with customers.

"Cut scope to get it delivered faster". Yeah, or just don't build the Rolls Royce directly, remember MVP (Minimum Viable Product). What is the least amount of work you can get away with to produce something that solves a problem?

CHAPTER 10

STARTING A PROJECT

Let's go from zero to hero by looking at the pieces needed for a Project that becomes a Product that becomes something useful.

You are going to build a great product, but I got news for you. It all starts as a project. It's fine. We can call it Product, MVP (Minimum Viable Product) or what we want, but it's going to start as a project first. Many companies are discussing the *why* and what the benefits of doing this particular activity would add. Check out Budget for some information about NPV (Net present value - what is it worth now?) —calculations and Build or Buy.

There are many Project management methodologies who can assist you in starting, planning, implementing, testing, releasing and closing your project. There are also some methodologies who runs this in iterations, ie short repeats, instead of longer "phases". What this means to projects has big implications to how you set it up, how you run it and how it's delivered.

For the sake of completeness of this little book, I will quickly explain classic Project management, aka "Waterfall". Imagine a river. This is your project process. You always move down the river and you are not going back to change things as you go, it's fixed and settled. So you move further and go in to different phases, like the implementation phase where all the code is supposed to be coded, and later the testing phase when it's supposed to be tested. Everything is based on up-front specifications that was written before your started the Project. You knew exactly what you wanted to build, down to the last button. So you spent months putting this in to a document, then your Senior developers or Architect helped you write the Functions in the Functional Specification document. Then in the Implementation phase you build exactly what was in this specification. Then you test that it's working like it was specified.

This has never ever worked in any tech projects. The best deliveries of these kind of projects produced an application that did exactly what it was intended to do, but did not take any findings or ideas in to consideration which was found during the development. Also, time passed during the Project duration, and you lost some chance to show this to a potential customer and get valuable feedback. You have now built something that you have not tested against any real user. I'm going to go out on a limb here and say that it's probably not going to be what you wanted.

■■

If you instead take the other approach, the Agile approach, it means you would be gathering something called User Stories which in effect are short specifications about your idea on how it should work, and you figure it out while you build the applications instead. This would give you a chance to see things being built "faster" and you can react on the results within small time-cycles. These are Agile iterations. You put all these user stories in a long list, and you put the most important things in the top, and you ask the developers how much they can finish within, say two weeks (this is called a Sprint). By doing this you bake in the entire estimation aspect, and once you get to know your team you can rely on how much they can eat from the Backlog (the list of tasks) in that Sprint. Sometimes you don't even need a Sprint, just that the developers can pick from the top whenever they want instead, when they are either waiting for input or getting stuck. There are _a lot_ more to say here about these approaches, but hey I said it was going to be to the point.

■■

In all approaches you would make some kind of Road map to understand what you want to do with the Project. This is a high level document or overview of, say 3-6 months, and has some of the bigger features or "solutions" listed in a calendar. Don't fall in to the trap of adding Milestones, or build a complete Gantt chart. There is no need. The Road Map will change 1000 times while you are going thru the project. A title and short description is enough, and place it under some kind of month. I'd even leave out length of it, as it would limit developers to some kind of time scoping.

One thing many classic Project has and has been very useful, is a Project Charter. It writes down, on a high level, what the project is about and when it's ready. In my opinion this is also not needed, but it doesn't hurt to not down a few points on what the project should achieve.

■■

When it comes to visualising the Backlog and the different statuses of a task or feature, I would recommend using a tool like Jira or Trello. It's easy to get an overview. In order to fully visualise the flow I would build out a Kanban board, which is a "To-do, Doing, Done"-board in columns, but with a few more statuses. More about that in Build a Product.

Starting a project starts with an idea of some solution to something, or a tool/system/online application etc that will make life easier for your users. The most important thing about your project is that you test and verify this idea of yours with real users as soon as possible. This, you can only do by building as little as possible, only what's needed to the absolute minimum in order to see if your customers likes it. This is the so-called MVP (Minimum Viable Product) approach. Gather the minimum things you need and build something as fast as possible (or with as little effort as possible) to be able to test this. This could even be a form! The entire idea here is to not get stuck in big features which takes a long time to build, but instead be able to adjust your idea quickly if you see that you have "traction" elsewhere, in a so called "pivot". Maybe one part of your idea gains more traction than your initial thoughts. Since you have (most likely) none or little data when you start your project, you are basing your entire idea on assumptions. And – since a person without data is just another person with an opinion, it's time to get the data. You need to validate your assumptions with your MVP. This can be done on tons of ways like focus groups, interviews etc etc but an easy way is to build something like an online application and send traffic to it via Google or LinkedIn ads. Or post the link in forums. Whatever brings traffic from (hopefully) interested potential customers. This is not a one-thing validation. It's iterative and goes on as long as you are working on the product. In the future, when you want to expand your idea/ application by adding new features, it's the same approach again; start small and build on the feedback. Feedback here is *conversion*. (Agile principle: *Working software is the primary measure of progress, Agile Manifesto (2001)*) I don't mean what people think or what they write, I'm talking about what people *do*. Buying, ordering, signing up, subscribing, downloading, using — any of these "Call To Actions" (CTA) are what drives conversion. The more of the right kind you have, the better your idea works. Simple as that. Don't fall in to the trap to develop/build things just because someone *thinks* it's going to work. Test early, adjust, release and see the effect.

CHAPTER 11

BUILD A PRODUCT

From idea to working product that actually is solving something for someone who's paying for it.

As you read in the Starting a Project chapter, building a project is all about trying out the idea fast and see how it's received, then build on the feedback (as in actions users do, not always what they say). With that little retrospective we continue the playbook for building a product. A short disclaimer: I'm not going to go in to pre-research such as Usability and User Experience (UX) as that is somewhat covered in the Agile chapter, and it's really another book, but let's mention that what your are building must look and feel good. Great interactivity at the right level. So get some good UX people aboard. It will make a huge difference. Leaving UX to Developers and Managers and it will look like an 1980s accounting system with 1000 buttons. So, no.

Ok, so provided you have a "nice design" (a UX designer would kill me for writing that) next thing to do is to choose which of the features are the least you need in order to make your product viable.

You have a great design mockup with tons of cool features. Say you are building an apartment listing website. You need login, subscribe to new advertisements, search filter, a way to add new listings, sharing them, adding photos, login logs, information pages, payment options for days of listing, admin user management, etc, etc. Which of these are core to the functionality of the application and which are not? All are core. So how do we pick out a few of these in order to build our MVP? Here you go — the most misunderstood thing in the entire MVP-approach is that you must choose "which features". You can build them all if you want, but you can't build them "fully" or "entirely". Take login as an example. You may not need to have the user use "forgot password" or set a 8 character super safe password or use Two Factor Authentication right away. That can come later. It may be enough with sending a "magic link" via email first. That even saves you the login page. For being able to add new listings, you just need a description field and a picture. Not very intuitive I agree, but you also don't want to spend your time here unless this is what makes your Product unique. And my guess is that it doesn't. Sharing? No need for fancy scripts, just display some social media icons and a link to the ad. The user can cut and paste themselves for now. Payment options? Nowadays a Stripe integration is simple, but why not just use a description field and ask the user for their address and send them an invoice instead. If they don't pay, remove their user access or call them and ask for feedback. This is just the beginning, it can be built out later. User management? Directly in the database. In this way you can build up a niche apartment listing website and test the concept early, before you take on risk and start burning money (yes it's called burn rate) until the first release. By working in small iterations that adds just one small addition to an existing feature or improves it, you are reducing waste in true Kanban style and the Toyota industrial engineer Taiichi Ohno would be proud of you.

The meaning of reducing waste is the mindset that all ideas, code or whatever is taking your time is waste until it's released to a production environment and is generating value. Take the example of the opposite. Imagine a form to generate lead information on your website. You are asking your users if they like your products and if they want more information. You come up with a great design of a form with questions about their experience and product needs etc. It takes 2 days to develop. You don't release what you have here, instead you work on the next iteration and add more things, all good so far. Then you show it to others in the organisation and get their input and you continue this process for what in reality is a month, a long back and forth. Now you have lost a month of getting leads on the website. If you instead would have released what you had working, as early as possible, then worked on the next iteration you would have gotten leads and continuously improved the form at the same time, and that without wasting the time in this case. You could argue that you do lose time during the process and you do waste some time rebuilding, but that's way less than holding it from being released for a long time. Extrapolate this to all features you are working on and you quickly see that leaving things not done and waiting for internal feedback and re-working without releasing it and gain the benefit of it, you lose not only a month but years of time where you could have something more simple working meanwhile. This is a blind spot for many micro managers and people who likes to sign off things, as important as they think they are, but in reality they can be a huge liability to the company and in the end cost hundreds of thousands of dollars extra. It's always a balance, but if something works and is adding value as it is, get it out the door sooner than later and work on the next iteration. You never know how many changes you get.

So for the next piece of the puzzle, in order to be able to accommodate an iterative Release Process, you need to set it up so that you can both work and release to different environments without long cycles and also with as less as dependencies as possible. Hence, workable tickets in say Jira, needs to ideally be small or as isolated as possible to avoid conflicts, or just change a small little thing.

For the Release Process, using a git repository is standard and what we can do to achieve a Kanban workflow as a Release Process is to use something called feature branches (in git). Basically (and hey here we get a bit "technical") we branch of from the Main branch (yes some calls it "master") and once done we make a Pull Request to the staging branch, with usual code reviews. Once approved it gets merged to staging and here we have an entire environment built on the staging feature branch which allows for "some" integration testing but mostly we can see and get the look and feel of our new feature. Provided the testing environment still works with standard test of forms and other features, and the feature works as good as it gets right now, we can now release it to a production environment by doing a Pull Request to the Main branch, again with code review and approval. The production environment is then based on the Main branch, so once the code is merged it will run there and this be "live". This is a much quicker release process than just releasing to a "Release train" with tons of other things, a code freeze, etc. Of course this works when you keep dependencies at bay (or release them at the same time). There will be conflicts on the testing environment but merging in main and resolving conflicts with conflict resolution branches bridges those problems.

So with having fixed the MVP-approach and the Release Process, you are now setup to move fast and furious with the product building. One last component is missing to make the process become truly learning and iterative.

As we build the product we are leaving the MVP and adding more features. As important as it is to add features to see how they are adopted and used, as important it is to also *remove* unused features. Crazy huh? Having leaner and less complex code make development faster, and if stuff is unused why keep it? Also you may decide to remove a feature if it's not bringing in enough revenue to justify keeping the development of it.

The key is to know what to keep, what to let go and when to fold*. That can be done by checking the analytics, user login behaviours, usage of the feature if available, interviews, interaction data, etc, etc.

*) "You got to know when to hold 'em, know when to fold 'em, know when to walk away, and know when to run...",
– Kenny Rogers, The Gambler, 1978

We talked a bit about mindset and development process, but building a product is a team work. It's not just about feeding Jira with ideas, it's about daring to explore new ideas that hopefully expands business or adds so much new value that users don't "fold" (gives up) or runs (leave) away. Knowing the users, analysing patterns and accommodating for better usage is keys to be successful in Product development. Not always is what the user wants the best for the company, so then question is if it should be built or not, or if we are better off building something else. Always a balance, but dare to try and see. No one knows. What didn't work a year ago may work now because of a change in the business environment, some political switch or some geopolitical winds. Demands and needs of users are ever changing and depends on feelings and we would all love to think they are rational, but they very seldom are.

To quickly touch "user needs" we can talk about hygiene factors. Imagine an employee coming to work. Having a desk to sit at, a chair, a power outlet for the computer adaptor and a reasonable stable indoor climate is a hygiene factor. The employee can't work without it, but is not happy that they have it. Same goes the other way around, the satisfiers are one thing and the Hygiene factors another. If you have a nice login button users will be happier (more satisfied) but if you don't have it they are not unhappy. (The opposite of satisfaction is not dissatisfaction)*

*) Herzberg's Motivator-Hygiene Theory (1950)

So it's a great exercise to divide users needs into what is seen as satisfiers and dissatisfiers. For example, having a great way of saving your searches may be seen as a satisfier while not having it may not be a dissatisfier. At the same time having an application that crashes is a dissatisfier and will make the users run away.

Timing, is another big deal, look at MySpace vs Facebook as interesting examples, of course done different and with the aforementioned with little network effect, still we don't search using MSN or AOL. We use Google (or DuckDuckGo). I don't think timing can be done so much about. Sure we can follow mega-trends and adjust, making best bets etc but it's better and more rewarding to just "do". One key take away of the entire discussion is that just because it *didn't* work before, it doesn't mean that it doesn't work now. Kind of an opposite but trying some ways with new fresh minds could be very rewarding.

Who decides what to build? Big question here and I'm going to jump to the end conclusion. The <u>business</u> does. In the end, what really matters from a company perspective, which is to maximise the value to the shareholders. Now, one can argue that this has slightly changed with many new environmental, health and humanist geopolitical initiatives but it still applies to a large extent.

In the end your idea must generate some kind of monetary value in terms of revenue, or do a great IPO.

"You never count your money, when you're sitting at the table, there be plenty of times to count, when the dealing is done."
– Kenny Rogers, The Gambler, 1978

Never stop developing new features and improve your product, as long as you increase sales and get new users. A short drop in user activities or sales doesn't mean that your product is losing relevancy. It means you need to keep improving and building a great product.

CHAPTER 12

PRIORITISING

What should you focus on now? I'm going thru some ways of creating value thru setting the right priorities.

Switching focus in the middle of the task is the worst thing for most developers, and perhaps also other employees. As a CTO or anyone leading developers your job is to either thru the Product Manager/Owner (or yourself if you take that role) setup a sustainable working environment which allows for employees to be able to contribute in a way that maximises the business value of their output. That sounded nice!

What I mean is that there are tons of task lists, boards, to-dos, follow-ups, excel sheets and ticket handling systems which tries to support business in project management and task handling. In fact I think there are too many.

■■

ONE LIST TO RULE THEM ALL

In the first book of Lord of The Rings (LOTR) – I promise to not make any other LOTR-references – we get introduced to the almighty powerful ring — one ring that will rule them all. In order to make business prioritisation - we need one list to rule them all. I'll explain why.

Many teams work different, with different priorities and sometimes for different stakeholders or "bosses". We tried to make the teams cross-functional but it quickly became evident that they needed to focus on one product in order to not have very long wait times for the other stakeholders. So we tried to focus everyone in a classic Agile Scrum Sprint. That worked as long as no other "boss" came in and asked someone in the team for something they needed "now" or until the employee was finished. Then what would they work on? They took up another task and wasn't ready until the Sprint was supposed to be delivered. That's a bit of background to why I recommend having a Backlog and working with Kanban. One list. Only one. Not two. One.

If we have one list, we can prioritise all the tasks coming in giving our stakeholders one view of it all, not different views. It will be honest and open. When we prioritise something higher we move things to the top. This forms then the consensus view of what we should be working on, agreed during a bi-weekly meeting with stakeholders. If I move some departments task up the priority, the other department can see their own tickets be less important. This is very useful as it gives food for discussion, reflection and justification and a "we" instead of trying to just get stuff done. Moving one thing before another always makes the other come after, no matter how you do it. Hence this exercise is the me most single important one to do.

Things will happen during the two weeks until the next meeting and if some emergency sails up that is indeed more important, the Product Owner can put it in the top of the list and it will be picked up by the developers, then explain the why to the relevant stakeholder in the next Prioritisation Meeting. In this way, everyone understands that they can't just get their stuff done now without someone else will have to wait.

If your organisation favours excel task lists or due dates, this is going completely against these agile principles. Having the most important stuff ready and workable in the top of the list means they will be worked on the next time a developer looks to pickup something new (they will never change what they are currently working on right now except in emergencies). This means it's more or less impossible to say exactly when things are done or when they will be release to production. It also involves testing and (hopefully) changes after the first draft solution which also adds time. So if things are time critical, better to do these items first and time the release of the ready feature instead of context changing the developers working flow.

Things that have higher prioritisation and should need a different process is emergencies such as 1) Site is down (we have no business) 2) Customers can't pay or order (we don't get any money). All the rest (including images and text changes to landing pages in ongoing campaigns) has to be prioritised accordingly. No shrimp sandwiches*.

*) Shrimp sandwich is a Swedish expression when someone gets to pass the queue and gets priority access.

CHAPTER 13

DEVELOPMENT PROCESS

How to get something from idea to done using a standard development process.

There are many different Development processes. I've worked with Waterfall phasing, scrum with sprints which releases all at the same time once done as well as Release Trains and all what they are called. The most superior Development process is the one that moves things from Idea to Done in the fastest and safest way possible. It can be called a lot of things, and have a lot of back thought like "reducing waste" and other actually less tangible names. We need to define what a Development process is. It's a process that moves ideas through different departments and people who needs to have a say, to people who codes them, to testing, to feedback, to changes, repeat and in the end to a release.

■■

As with all other topics in this book, we can't just dive in to the development process without talking about the **why** (Simon Sinek would be proud).

We want to be able to react to feedback from our users quickly. We also want to be able to build new features that will increase the usage and therefore the revenue of our product. We also want to make sure that when we introduce new things, other things shouldn't break. At the same time we want to be able to test new things and see how they are adapted. We want to focus on what's most important now but also not change focus and move away from finalising what was important yesterday and still now delivered. We don't want a mayhem entropy where things gradually decline into disorder. Keeping creativity high, enabling instead of limiting employees. So we have a Development Process. Sounds like a lot? How can a process enable creativity, isn't it the other way around? On an axis of opposites you have creativity on one side and process on the other? The answer: It depends. It's again a balance. Too strict and there will be now creativity. Let's dive in.

I like to divide the process in to a few "stages" in which an idea moves until done.

Idea Stage: This stage captures all ideas from anyone in the company. These could be short ideas or big ideas which can be discussed at some idea or brainstorming meeting. As everyone can create these ideas, it's also a way of keeping the product development open. How things gets transitioned from this stage depends, maybe it's by upvoting or just qualified by the Product Owner.

Request stage: Normally all requests lands here; bugs, changes, new features. It's the capture lane for everything that employees or leaders wants to have done. A well captured issue contains a screenshot, a short description and a url. The person who is behind requests is called the Reporter, and champions the ticket throughout the process.

Backlog stage: Only gone thru, well understood and checked tickets can come to this stage, and only moved by the Product Owner, or whoever has the role. Once moved over, they are prioritized from the top and down. Developers will pick from the top to the extent they can, however they choose to work on (another great motivator). No one except of the Product Owner is allowed to re-prioritise or move things in to this stage. It's worth repeating.

In Progress stage: From this stage, the developers are themselves responsible to move the ticket to Done. This helps with the entire process, as the developer will accommodate and move it forward as they want to be done. So there is no reassigning happening. Assigned is the lead developer who picked up the ticket. Multiple developers can work on the same ticket, but the assignee is never changed. The developers shares information with the rest of the team every day in the form of a stand-up meeting and answers the three scrum questions: 1) What have I done until today? 2) What will I do until tomorrow and 3) Do I have any issues I need help with.

Blocked stage: If a developer can't move forward, the ticket is moved to the Blocked stage. There could be missing content, needing to wait for a Reporter or the solution is not found. Putting something in the Blocked stage in a Kanban project means it's highly visible that something is not moving like it should, and should be take care of.

Testing stage: Once a ticket is merged to a staging or testing environment, the Reporter gets invited to help testing it. It's manually sanity checked and pre-tested by the developer before and this should be the default behaviour of any developer. Personally, I don't wan't to move away the responsibility from the developer to a QA (Quality Assurance)-team, which takes longer. But for some larger and more complex testing it could be needed and be faster. Automated testing is also performed.

Done stage: Once something is merged to the main branch and thus released to production, it is set to done. This is a clear definition of Done.

– "Wow you just described an old school project, it's not agile!" Hold on a bit, what we have here allows for individual ideas/tickets to move thru the process independently from the other ones. That's the main difference. Also, we can move back and forth any time we want for any valid reason. This can't be compared to the waterfall project with all its dependencies and testing issues. We can change requirements any time and add new functionality if we like. So this is true agile. What could be missing is the collaboration between developers, as they tend to focus on just "their" ticket.

Tech warning*, we are getting advanced here.* From a git (hub or lab or any other) perspective the development process is very similar.

1. Main branch

2. Dev pulls latest update from the Main branch
   git checkout main
   git pull
   git checkout -b feature-branch

3. Dev works on feature branch locally

4. Dev stages and commits changes to their branch
   git add
   git commit -m "Message with ticket number"
   git push

5. Dev makes a Pull Request (PR) to the staging branch and adds the peer reviewers.
   (if conflicts, merge in staging branch and solve conflicts in a stage-merge-branch which can be deleted)

6. PR is being reviewed

7. PR is approved and merged, ticket is set to Testing (stage)

8. Once testing is done either there are changes and process repeats from 3-5 or it is OK to release and then the dev makes a PR to main branch, adding peer reviewers.

9. Once the branch is approved and merged, it will be closed (deleted). The code is now a part of the main branch and can be pulled by other devs.

Sometimes the staging (or test) branch needs to get Main merged to avoid increasing conflicts.

CHAPTER 14

BUILD OR BUY

SaaS or develop yourself?

The classic question that you have heard so many times, in so many shapes. Now, slightly adjusted for our purpose I will discuss some thoughts around the topic.

If you want to build the most expensive tool ever built — build it yourself. It's the most costly way of getting it done. Not only because you are most likely re-inventing the wheel — that has no real cost except "opportunity cost" (the cost of not doing the second best option — classic finance term) — but because of the fact that you do need to develop, then maintain, and o top of that you need to build ALL functionality yourself. *Nothing* is "out-of-the-box". However - if the system doesn't exist — what to do? And further, today no one just starts coding from scratch, there are frameworks, open source libraries, vendor folder management, tons of packages, and platforms as a service.

Another very expensive way of building your "tool" is to buy something third party, like your favourite Sales CMS, and then "customise it". Many are the companies that lives off from these customisations, that are in themselves hidden mega projects sometimes designed to make the most profit for these “Service Partners”. “Out-of-the-box” or “Off-the-shelf” rarely works the way you wanted it work. However, no one in their right mind would build their own accounting system nowadays, right? There are tons of them out there and they are semi automated even. Some even claims AI (when this book was written, there were still no awakening self-awareness of any artificial intelligence known). The point I’m trying to make is that most likely you can get a decent accounting system that does what is should for a small subscription fee. There's no point in developing it yourself. Unless you have a new awesome idea on how to make the next much better accounting system out there of course.

I’m not even going to mention buying classical software licenses and hosting something on premise. Just *don’t* do it.

■■

Systems for just accounting, salary payments, credit card payments etc are probably easiest to get “third party”.

When it comes to you building your product that you are going to sell to your customers, I must say that it's a good idea to of course first scan the market for similar solutions, but then probably you are better off building it yourself. This is your main product! You can do it better. You also don’t want to be stuck with some way of doing it, and not being able to change the core of the systems or add new functionality on your own. So here I think it's best to build.

To test your MVP idea, of course the best features are the ones never built — meaning the more you don't build (develop) — the cheaper it gets — as in you find other cheaper ways to test if your product and evaluate the results — the better you can focus on the right things. So in testing mode — try whatever is out there.

There are a lot of exceptions here. Like if you are working in a huge company, getting everyone licenses to Salesforce may cost 100s of thousands. Plus the "configurations" (consultant hours). So there is a business case here to be made — of course you can't replicate the functionality of Salesforce - but do you really need all those features? Maybe it's "cheaper" to build your own basic "database" with a simple UI on top? Back to MVP and try to see what the features are that's really going to be used vs "needed". Today it's also much easier to develop quality applications (and maintain them) than before.

TECH

Get your nerdy glasses on! The next section goes in to the actual coding – the art of building something by using programming languages, make it look in a certain way for a user and then deploy it to a server. Buckle up!

CHAPTER 15

CODING

99% of developers would not call Software development "coding". We input instructions in a file, which is interpreted by another program on the server, returning back a result. That's it.

Coding is indeed the art of telling the "computer" what to do according to certain conditions. What coding *really* is, is that it is a bunch of 1's and 0's in a long stream. The processor reads these *binary* codes like "on" and "off" and performs computation based on what the binary code means. Each of these 1's and 0's are called "bits" and they can be grouped in sections of 8 which are called "bytes".

Let's write "hello". This would in binary code (ASCII) be:

01101000	01100101	01101100	01101100	01101111
H	E	L	L	O

It's important to understand this, as we are not really "coding" binary strings. We are instructing a program to give us a certain results. There are some layers of code interpreters that does the heavy lifting of translating this down to the processor. Let's leave that right there. When we are talking about coding, developers have installed a so called development environment on their computers. They get all the folders and files from a "git repository" which means they can download all the code of the product to their own computer. They view the files and edit them in so called "IDE's" (Integrated Development Environments). Nowadays they may not be so integrated anymore, as depending on which programming language you work with, there may be many things you need to have installed on your computer to make it possible to run and see the code performing what you told it to in a web browser.

Now that the developers can see all their files, they can edit them and see the result. This is the process of coding. Let's visualise one simple example.

In the url field of the web browser, there are sometimes many things after the url. Like https://awesome.com/?message=hello. We can tell the program to use the variable "message" and display ("print") the contents:

```
If ($message) {
echo $message;
}
```

This is basically saying "if we have the variable message and it's not empty, we want to do this: print the variable message". This was a very basic way to visualise coding. This example is in PHP, a popular Programming Language.

The developers also most likely will need a database installed on their computer, so they can organise data in columns and rows, and choose to create, read, update or delete it (so called "CRUD") based on the operations of the software they are building.

Once the developers have coded what they needed, they will *push it* to a certain git branch. This is a way to maintain the code and make it easy to share between developers.

Now, this code can be deployed to a testing server. It's similar to the "local" setup the developers have, but it has things installed that are more optimised and setup in a certain way that makes it focused on running the code, without anything else on the server. Here, you can use Docker, which is essentially a little "container" with some settings of a server; how much RAM, how much hard drive space and how much CPU. You can host your code in there, both on the local computer but also on servers. I'm just letting you in on the lingo here, I'm not going to explain more about Docker, Nginx and the many things surrounding this concept.

When it's all tested, the code will move to a Production server. The steps are similar as above. The true definition of when something is Done, is when it's released to the Production (also usually called Live) server.

CHAPTER 16

PROGRAMMING LANGUAGES VS FRAMEWORKS VS STACKS

Here we are discussing programming languages, frameworks and stacks.

Software development in the context of this book means building an application that is used in the web browser. Or, in some cases, on your phone as an installed "app". While traditional applications, also known as Desktop Applications, may still have their use in some places, that's not what the majority of companies are building anymore. (Yes, Adobe and Microsoft are still delivering desktop applications to be installed on your computer). For the sake of this book, we are talking about Cloud-hosted applications.

Many of the programming languages existed a long time before web was popular, and was somewhat grown from that history in to become more "web-friendly". It's very different to code a desktop application in comparison to a web application. A web application is not a website, even though it works similar.

Some of the most popular programming languages include Python, JavaScript, Java, C#, C, C++, Go, R, Swift and PHP. When it comes to coding web applications, Python and JavaScript are widely used. Larger ones usually use .Net (C#), Java or PHP. Mobile applications are usually written in Swift (iOS) or Kotlin (Android), but this is not always the case.

These days, no one in their right mind would just start coding "from scratch". Most likely, they will use a *framework*. A framework organises the code structure in to certain folders (called MVC - Model, View, Controller) as well as folders for css (stylesheets) and images etc. A common structure makes the coding life much easier and developers don't have to reinvent that wheel, at least for this.

Common frameworks are Express (Node.JS), Django (Python), Rails (Ruby), Laravel (PHP), Spring (Java), Angular (Typescript), React (front end library) and Vue.js (JavaScript).

Most of the frameworks include things like login and user management, REST API, translations, web routing (url handling), cache handling, better ways to talk to the database, vendor script package management and can thus be seen as a kind of boiler plate to get you started faster.

Web servers that are widely used include Apache, Nginx and IIS.

The commonly used databases are MS SQL, MySQL/MariaDB, PostgresSQL and MongoDB. They are different mainly as SQL is a "classic" columns/rows type of relational database while a NoSQL (not only SQL) uses keys values, documents (XML, JSON, YAML).

Stacks are a name to describe which programming language, framework, database and sometimes scripts the application is using. Popular stacks are MEAN, MERN or MEVN (Mongo, Express , Node and either Angular, React or Vue), Ruby on Rails, Flutter and LAMP (Linux, Apache, MySQL, PHP).

There are many more combinations of tech stacks, and not always abbreviated. Companies write their tech stack in job ads as well and may then include which specific open source frameworks or certain scripts are used.

A somewhat new framework is Ionic, in which you code either in Angular or React, and can then "build" (make a deliverable package) it in to a mobile application, either for iOS (Apple) or Android (Google). This means you can code your application for both Google Play Store and Apple Store just using *one* code base (more or less). This is very powerful, as maintaining multiple code bases is expensive, may require different skills from the developers and will require the functionality to be built twice. The experience from an app built like this may not 100% be a *Native*, meaning as if it was built using Kotlin or Swift. But it can certainly be a good alternative. With the ionic framework you can also use native functionality such as the camera, upload files, login etc.

Today's world of programming languages, frameworks, scripts, databases and stacks are very diverse and it can be hard to navigate and decide which one to use. Maybe the developers are also suggesting to use a new one. New frameworks can take your application to the next level, and usually have many great things built in that you before needed to do manually. But, just changing for the sake of changing costs a lot of time and effort, and it's not entirely sure that this is what is the true business need. On the other hand, not testing new things and evolving, will make you stuck where you are. It's also hard to attract talented developers if they are not allowed to try new things and work on their cool new framework. That's one side. The other side is that some of the frameworks are not longer maintained and you can't get new updates anymore, so your code base will slowly be outdated, which could lead to security and compatibility issues.

CHAPTER 17

FRONTEND & BACKEND AND THEIR DEVS

What happens in the browser, stays in the browser.

We divide code in Frontend and Backend. Not really for fun, but because of a reason. In order to understand basic Software Architecture, we need to understand the split between frontend and backend. It's not so easy as to say that what you see is the frontend and the backend is just "everything behind". We need to think about server side and client side. So, code is running on a server. When an online application is loading (it's requested) first some things are happening on the server side, then the output of this (whatever is "calculated") lands in a browser. This is the frontend. End of story? Not so fast. Before CSS (stylesheets) and JavaScript was first introduced, the web was very much backend driven. Every page was reloaded with a new request and sent from the server to your browser. Although fast, it always required refresh of the page every time something new was done. With the entrance of JavaScript, a lot of interactions happened directly in the browser. Now we wanted these "events" to talk to the backend, without refreshing the entire page and reload everything. So hello Ajax calls. And welcome jQuery. But it quickly got messy and along came Angular and React. Complete frameworks which helps building fast JavaScript based applications. Then hello Node.js. A backend environment that runs JavaScript (frontend).

Digging deeper is out of scope. I will switch to share my experiences working with frontend, backend and full-stack developers instead.

■■

Frontend developers knows how to move from an idea to a complete interactive piece of code using HTML/CSS/JavaScript, etc. Asking a frontend developer to fix something in the backend is like asking a carpenter to renovate your bathroom. They could figure it out, but it will take a while.

Backend developers know how to architect an application from the database model, to controllers, routes and API's. They are most likely experts in PHP, Java, .Net, Python or any other or many programming languages. Asking a backend developer to fix the frontend, is like asking the building architect to paint your house. They could also figure it out, but it will take a while.

We also got some full-stack developers. This means they know the entire code stack, meaning both backend and frontend. Is that true? Yes and no. I've met developers that always leaned to one side stronger, which you could see in how they solved issues — using their preferred coding method. I've also met awesome developers who does both without any issues. Is it a bit ambidextrous? Perhaps, but new school coding means knowing both.

CHAPTER 18

DEVOPS

The important work of maintaining servers, environments, code bases, version and all to enable developers to work.

Development Operations. This guild that few knows the essence of. Is it just a developer fixing some automatic release scripts? Yes, sometimes. Is it sometimes a person planning server usage time and buying spots on AWS according to a forecast to get the price down for high usage applications? Is it a person who takes a backup of the database? Ensuring SSL-certificates are updated? Yep, could be.

Many developers are also good at devops. They can setup servers and create build scripts. But for a more manageable approach with clear responsibility (and expertise), look to get a Devops manager on your team.

■■

A Devops person is someone who has the responsibility to ensure the developers have what they need in order to be able to continue to develop, test and release the application they are working on. The developers works on something called a "Developer environment" which is first of all a fast computer with a lot of RAM-memory (the newer and better the computer is, the faster it takes for the application to *build* or *compute*), and IDE (Integrated Development Environment) which is a software to do coding in, a "localhost" which is a server on the developers computer where code can run, a database can be hosted and it can be seen in a browser. Then, there are tons of add-ons to that. You may want to use Docker to "containerise" your localhost meaning setup a virtual server which gets virtual resources from your computers in terms of CPU, memory, disk, etc. This helps from eating the entire computers resources. Or you may use some other VM.

Was this heavy? *Find out more in the Coding chapter.*

The Devops role here is to make it easy for developers to get up and running the development environment locally on their computer. I've always used this as a KPI for how good a development process is. If a developer is up and running within a day — it's very good. Takes a week? (I have seen this) — not so good. Just putting instructions into a readme-file is not very helpful, it needs to be supported well. Devops are also monitoring the server usage in terms of resource usage, and need to be able to scale if needed, by adding more resources or push back to developers to build more efficient code. I'm a fan of not "departmentalise*" devops, but instead embed, which means devops is a part of the team and a valued colleague which the entire team can access.

**) Departmentalise something and you've invented new KPIs, team targets and a "us and them" mentality. Server CPU % becomes more important that supporting released as it screws up KPIs.*

Setting up automatic testing and builds between localhost git branches, testing servers and production servers, maintaining code integrity and vendors (external scripts), prettify code, setting up code quality processes – the list of tasks are long.

For an organisation - depending on the scale – having either a developer being "Devops" or a pure devops is key to be able to deliver great code. Servers, Performance and Availability is one thing, making sure developers can actually develop is another. If you have the Kanban development flow blocked, nothing will come out of the production line.

CHAPTER 19

TESTING

Well, you don't want obvious bugs. Releasing fast doesn't mean we need to release things that breaks the application or looks bad.

To test something before release is a good idea. Testing is as with everything else — a big topic and there are different schools on how to do it. We are obviously not talking about a "testing phase" here a la old school project management. To wait to test everything until the end of a project may come off as hilarious today, but it was a common practice and still is in many Waterfall projects. Luckily most have moved on. Wait with testing and the developers have moved on and forgotten and it's almost a new project to fix all the small things. Today companies use continuous testing which needs to happen in a testing environment before the ticket/story/fix goes to production (gets released). In this way, we can code features, test them, give feedback, code again and continue testing until we are happy with the result. We can release whenever it's ready on a per-feature basis.

In many development processes the developer codes something, then tests a bit on their local computer and then commit the code and make a Pull Request for peer review (in the best case). Then it's on the testing environment. Here, some developers like to hand over to a QA ("Quality assurance") team that takes over the testing responsibility and "make sure" that it has "the right quality". This looks good on the paper. Don't do it! At least not like that.

■■

Giving someone else than the developer the full responsibility for the ticket is a great way to un-empower developers and to mess up with the **definition of done**. Also, it'll not move your tasks ahead. At all. Instead it creates an "us and them" and a "let's throw stuff over the hedge" (for someone else to care about). The first thing the QA-team will ask here is "what have you built" and the next is "how should it work" and all good so far but they are not asking over Slack or in the ticket. They are asking by making developers fill out request forms in their ticket systems, with standardised texts. They also need to the prioritise what they should test now, and they also need to manage their request from other teams. This takes a lot of time from both the developer and increases the need for new processes. This leads to longer development time.

Let the developer who developed the ticket stay responsible from In Progress until Done. Done means "it's released to production and it's creating value for a user. It could be heavy for developers to test, but the process is self cleaning; they will build less complex code and will test better themselves. You can think of embedding a QA-person in to the team that all developers can take help from for some more repetitive bigger testing like “is our main forms still working?” and testing of application core functionality. In this way the developers are still responsible. I’m also a fan of involving the rest of the organisation as in –*“Business people and developers must work together daily throughout the project.” (Read more in the Agile chapter).* Business people understands the user and will test it like a user, meaning not only technically. Does it make sense to have the feature like this? Does it look nice? Is it understandable? A second opinion is not bad to have. Working with true agile product development allows for changes all the time. That’s a good thing.

Then we have the big topic of automated testing. Of course you should do it. It's a core part of development, and hands on the heart we (all devs that is) did TDD (Test Driven Development) before someone invented the acronym. It’s a nice name for “build something, break it, fix it”. But, and here is a hot potato — more testing, even automated, make things take longer. Yep, it does. Maybe it should take longer and not doing it for some may mean you skip an important step. Sure. But hey — business first. For larger applications it’s a must, I’d say — but who am I to tell you how to do it. I can just tell you how I did it. I had that embedded QA person, who also used Selenium in the browser to some extent, then we setup some form testing from Pingdom which could tell us if the form didn’t have the right elements. Sometimes it's what’s simple and easy that wins.

I have seen the difference when developers were kept responsible and were able to move a ticket from idea to production. They were asking other team members for help and were very proud when they were able to get stuff out the door themselves.

One extra note, which is more of a mindset than any practice, I'd say that of course things need to be tested, but if you have a too long process where devs must build special test code, then the peer reviewer also tests, then you need to holler up the QA team and get on their list, then fix whatever they found — this could potentially add weeks and sometimes months. Is it then worth it? At which point did we leave the MVP path? This depends a lot on your application size, but it's healthy anywhere to not have rigorous strict processes that just takes a lot of time.

CHAPTER 20

MAINTAINING THE CODE

Git, Pull Requests, Quality, Workflows, Four-Eye-Principle, Prettify –

As mentioned in the previous chapter, Devops are important to maintain code but guess what this is also a team effort, and on top of that it's also a business critical priority, because with bad code comes bad things.

Coding "Free for all" meaning developers just develops how they feel like is far far away from how the code should be maintained in a great product code repository.

One of the overlooked "why's" here is that the code is Intellectual Property (IP) owned by the company and has a monetary value if not in the accounting books then as a possible asset value if the company is sold. That alone makes it worth to keep the code maintained.

Further – why is it that the code should be readable and overview-able? The most important functions should be documented, at least high-level (it is extremely hard to keep documentation updated in a rapid development environment, and could slow down development a lot).

Having the code in a git repository ensures new versions can be added and you can always go back and track what was added by who, and if you used a task management system to manage your Backlog you can also track the ticket or task behind, making for a very good documentation of history. This is useful to see why something was changed and what triggered it. By working in branches the developers have their own distributed copy of the code on their own computer and can collaborate easily by pulling an update of the code if another developer has been working on either the same branch or if new feature branches was added to the main branch during a production release.

A Pull Request is when a developer wants to ask a colleague for a peer review of their code. They are asking "can you look if my code is ok to be merged to the test branch" (which in this example has the test environment). The reviewing developer looks at the Pull Request and can leave comments, ask for changes or decline the PR. If it's a big branch, the reviewer downloads (pulls) the entire branch to their development environment and checks it out locally. What's important to mention here it to avoid reviewers to be some kind of gate keeper or someone up the hierarchy. The reviewer should be a colleague as this is a "peer review" from someone on "the same side". Otherwise these reviews will take forever and could potentially go on into absurdum.

Also, the mentions and findings of the reviewer should be helpful and pointers, not rules one must follow. It's all a balance. But if you have a super strict review process, nothing will move and it will become a bottleneck, doing more harm than well. This is of course debatable. There are many different angles in to this, but in the end we must build what the business needs. One usual feedback from reviewers, apart from using right variables or functions, is that code should be easy readable and "prettified". It sounds trivial but it's important the code is formatted in a consistent way. This will save time for the next developer to update or change the code again.

When it comes to Pull Requests to the main branch, which then deploys the code to the production application, it's also important to do another review again. This is called a Four-Eye-Principle and used to once again check that things are ok before a release. I'm not mentioning the testing here, which is part of the Release Process and Testing chapters.

Ensuring the right people have access to the code repository using their own named accounts is also crucial, especially if it's a private project.

Another aspect of code maintenance is all the dependencies we have between scripts, code and packages. In modern applications, these reside in a "vendor" folder and is somewhat easy to keep updated. But this was not always the case. Updating to certain versions of a package could create a chain-reaction and other things stops from working anymore. That's why also these changes are tested in the local and test environment before being released to production.

Keeping the framework and server versions up to date also helps. Some frameworks takes major leaps in their versions, and it can be complicated to upgrade. As discussed in the Programming Language chapter, this is very important but it's a balance of when it should be done and how much of the dev teams efforts should go to it. This is a crucial part of Devops.

■■

CHAPTER 21

DOCUMENTATION

At the right level at the right moment

Bring out your favourite pillow because it's time for some discussion about everyones most boring topic — documentation. Believe it or not, in the beginning of dev times this was a true and an important deliverable. Documentation was (and still is in some industries) a separate profession. What's the purpose nowadays? Of course to make it easier for developers to understand how the application works, before changing it, and without the need to spend weeks trying to backwards engineer code.

I'm going to be super blunt in order to save your time. There is really no need to have detailed documentation anymore. If you are using standard frameworks, these are already documented by whoever is maintaining them, and that alone takes you far. Secondly, no one will read it. Sorry, they won't. So it's a much better idea to focus on documenting parts of the code which are complex, contains heavy business logic and which performs some important function in your application. A 3-5 pages long document describing the functionality in a high level way, with details about statuses or what it may be — will be read because it's comprehensive and easy to grasp quickly. All documentation needs to be maintained, so once you are done coding some complex logic for a feature, it's a good idea to brain dump down the most important things about it. You will thank yourself later.

■■

Some argues that code is self-explanatory and in itself a documentation. In a way it is — but it will take time to read thru an applications code base and only when you are really poking at it with a stick (you are coding and testing) it will respond and you wish you had that little high level document stored.

There are ways to add comments in the code and follow some great standards like PHPDoc (for PHP) but it's important to remember that we should write what the code is supposed to do, not what it does. We also need a why and how to use it.

Another tip is to have textedit (or notepad) open and write some pointers as you develop. Procrastinating your documentation and saving it until after you are done coding will most likely lead to it never getting done.

CHAPTER 22

DATA

You capture a lot, but why do you need it?

Data is the new oil, I used to hear when I worked as an Agile Coach at Maersk Digital in Copenhagen. True that, but it's not new. Data is important and interpreted in a way that makes sense, it could help your company to take the right decisions. During the recent years there has been a lot of new regulation regarding the handling of data which has also of course made its way in to the architecture and structure of both coding and database decisions.

Basically it's simple; private data about users (including traceable links to a person) with their address, telephone number, images, activities etc can only be kept if the company has the users consent and only of there is a need for it. There are enough information about this out there to be able to find which Article in which regulation to reference to, but it's important to remember that not only do you need to only hold relevant data from the users if it's OK with them, you also must safe guard it from being used for anything else.

■■

This means having clear data handling processes. The user has the right to be forgotten if they are no longer your customer and you have no ongoing business, which would take a higher priority, (at least according to GDPR) so you cannot have users personal data laying around in excel files, various systems and also share them back and forth. How can you then delete it if the user asks for it? Key here is to understand that user personal data is not your data, it's owned by the user.

One solution to deletion of data is to make a soft delete, and anonymise/scramble the user personal data. In this way the user data itself are nonsense, but the transactions can still be seen, just not connected to any person. Then it's fine to keep and this still makes your report being able to aggregate important information about user behaviours.

Sharing sensitive data with external parties also needs the users consent, and the parts needs to sign a Data Processing Agreement as well as having correct processes in place to keep the data safe. Password-protect anything that's going to be sent via email, Slack or even Google Drive and the likes. There are great services like onetimesecret.com which can be used to share passwords.

Cookies are one of the most misunderstood pieces of information which has led some users to think that cookies holds evil information about them which is shared to everyone. This is not true, but nevertheless users ideally don't want them. Without cookies, some websites can't function properly as they move through different states and tries to remember what the users clicked on and not. There are workarounds though. Many companies uses the cookie consent form which is covering a big part of the screen when you come to a website. Also, they make it possible to deselect some services/scripts and also cookies. It's however disturbing the user experience. Many browsers takes care of this already. Safari and DuckDuckGo already blocks things by default. So it's becoming increasingly hard for marketeers to track users.

Using order, booking, product, purchase, status and event data you can make interesting analysis of your data and create reports, which can be used to forecast, plan or find important events. The events can be used to understand the user behaviour and further help you understand where you are profitable, and where you are not.

If most of your orders comes during the evening, and you also have a lot of abandoned orders then, it could be a valid conclusion that having the user being able to chat with customer representatives during their purchase could be a way to increase orders.

If you see that many of your customers orders by phone, it could be a valid assumption that your order process is not good enough and users find it easier to call.

If you get a sudden spike in calls instead of online orders, it could be a good idea to look at if this user target group is profitable enough to justify the more expensive and manual activity of taking calls.

This comes under the roof of Business Intelligence (BI) and some companies has entire departments looking at this. It's good to use some visualisation tool to share around insights from. It's no understatement that building up a good data structure which makes it possible to draw conclusions could be mean a great advantage.

It's also becoming increasingly popular to build self learning algorithms that gets better and better at predicting and suggesting activities or actions. Machine Learning can help us analyse data and present it in new ways to learn much more. So having data to analyse is usually good. Having huge databases with old and irrelevant data, maybe not.

CHAPTER 23

MONITORING

Keeping all your applications properly monitored makes it easier to understand if they are up or down.

Astonishingly many online services are not monitored and this has the obvious effect that no one knows when they are working or not. An important tool in the box would be an online uptime monitoring application like Pingdom or Better Uptime. It can check the uptime every minute by sending pings to your website or service. Using apps it can help many tech leaders to be able to be reactive and invoke incident management processes when things are down.

■■

Monitoring services can also help doing online testing against important forms or elements, by checking if they are accessible in the code.

Monitoring applications servers CPU, Memory and Disk usage can usually be done in the management consoles of the cloud server providers, and it's a good idea to make alerts and or policies on how to act on the alerts. If the database is full, it can't be written to anymore and this means no new orders coming in for example. Not good. Seeing alerts means it can be reacted to early and dealt with, instead of leading to an incident.

Company wide employee usage of sensitive files, download and sharing behaviours can be audited i.e. in Google Drive (Google Workspace) as well as in Office 365. This can lead to valuable insights to prevent data leak, unauthorised usage or sharing activities.

CHAPTER 24

INCIDENT MANAGEMENT

When the shit hits the fan

Late Friday evening, just when you are about to sit down for that family dinner, the phone buzzes and you get notifications from your favourite monitoring service that the website is down. You excuse yourself and prepare for a complete night of fixing whatever needs to be fixed.

Lesson number one in Incident management is: **avoid it**. Implement release windows that doesn't release anything to production in evenings or after Friday lunch. Nothing is worse than having to spend the weekend (in the best case) to fix some new bug or start your laptop on Monday morning just to realise an entire weekend of uptime and hence no sales or the service is gone. No one is there to fix it, so you need to scramble together some developers that are unfortunate enough to respond to your calls and WhatsApp messages. Once you are all online you spend the night fending off the obvious question from Product Owners, Manager, Co-workers, Stakeholders, Customers or your family — "when is it fixed?"

Or, you can have a written Incident Management process which still needs people to do some work, but clearly takes care of the entire incident in a responsible, manageable and outcome-driven way. By having a rotating schedule of developers in a call-chain, no one has to be available all the time or sit and wait for issues. But if the, yeah stuff, hits the fan then you are ready. Because it will. Once the process is activated it is as important that stakeholders are trained and understand that there is a process and the issue is being worked on, no matter how fast they want the issue resolved. They need to respect the process, in order to avoid mayhem, blaming, conflicts and "he said-she saids". And most importantly, to get it fixed.

Incident process:

1. An incident comes in and gets validated as a real incident. A very valid step here is the validation. Text changes or image changes are not incidents. If customers can't order or pay, it's an incident.

2. An Incident manager is appointed. This person communicates updates and keeps everyone informed (preferably in a dedicated Slack channel). No one except the Incident manager is allowed to talk to the developers. No one needs to hear how important it is to fix the service constantly, or receive threats to what happens if it's not fixed "asap".

3. The Incident manager calls in developers using the call chain. If it's during day time it's all hands on deck, everyone jumps in and roll up their sleeves (provided the incident is that important).

4. Once a fix is found, the release process is completely bypassed. The only thing that matters here is to fix the issue in the production servers. We can fix the rest later.

5. If the problem is solved, the Incident Manager informs everyone and the case is closed.

6. The next available working day, a Root Cause Analysis (RCA) meeting is held where the bug gets discussed, a possible root cause (late release, lack of test, stressed out fix, low quality code or unpredictable event etc) is identified and fixed according to priority.

7. Report back findings and write a nice communication to the rest of the company outlining what happened, why, and how things like this are going to be avoided in the future.

CHAPTER 25

API'S

Get data from other sources using API's.

Finally something fun! Application Programming Interface (API) is the way to connect different systems with each other. Is it plug and play as in you just click and it's done? No way. 99% of all API's require programming and setups. But in the end, an API is like a url that you can see in the browser, all those ?yes=1&no=2 etc actually means something (REST/HTTP). Without going in to more technical details, API's are also products. There are tons of API's you can subscribe to which you can get all sorts of information from: currency exchange rates, stock prices, vendor prices, images, content, company info — you name it.

What's really good about API's is that you can make them secure by using passwords (keys) which means the sending is encrypted and protected. You can monitor them and you can scope them, which means you can get what you need and ignore the rest. This is a huge step away from how it was back in the days. CSV-files containing data was uploaded to ftp-servers or databases was directly connected to each other.

■■

Some are afraid of API's, thinking it'll take a long time to develop and that it's super complex. It's not. Most API's have good documentation available and you can easily see how you can make certain calls and what you can get back. Some API's even offer code examples so it's easy to implement. However – all API's needs to be maintained. In our ever changing online environment, constant improvements are being done, so also to API's. So there will be new features added to these kind of products too.

In a continuously developing world stuff gets changed all the time. So it's a good idea to monitor the calls and set up alerts which gets emailed if it's not working. And even though the technology (in this example REST) is pretty standard, of course the properties and variables in the actual API's are not. Hence, if you are going to make changes, it's a good idea to keep some basic documentation available.

For those completely new to API's, have a look at Postman(.com) and Swagger(.io).

CHAPTER 26

COMPUTERS AND SECURITY

Infrastructure, antivirus, azure, office 365, drive, client management — all those IT tasks.

Is IT-management a part of the work as a CTO? Sound more like something under the wings of a CIO – but in reality in smaller companies the CTO could need to do this. At the minimum a good strategy for using computers, sharing files, handling licenses etc should be setup.

Short history lesson: Back in the days employees got a ready installed computer (desktop), without admin access and a user so they could log in to the "domain". Those were the days. The IT-department could keep all computers Windows's updated and everyone was happy. The corporate procurement departments bought "company computers" which had replaceable parts, good be serviced, had on demand replacement (onsite) and was easy to reinstall when needed. The computers came in batches and the manufacturing companies promised "long cycles" which meant they kept spare parts available.

■■

Did this every work practically? I doubt it. What it did was to limit users by not letting them install anything, and dooming them to slow computers that was stuck in a "batch" and whenever they got an issue they couldn't do anything themselves as the IT department needed to login as admins to fix it. So again we created tons of work for no reason. Did I mention the computers were slow too? That prompted the managers to get faster, smaller, lighter and of course unsupported computers for themselves. Another way to distinguish important managers from the staff crowd. This never worked for developers — as it took a second before someone needed to run some shell command in terminal, and hence needed admin access. Also, a developer computer must be fast and have a lot of memory — not to impress subordinates — but to make the code calculations faster and hence not needing to wait for builds or whatnot (wheel of doom). In any case — the dream from the IT department to control computers was at best a good attempt to streamline and standardise, and at the worst costed the company tons of money for nothing.

Nowadays, there are established concepts like BYOD "Bring your own device". Still frowned upon and sometimes blocked from the IT department, it's a concept where employees uses their own computers at work. They can also be owned by the company. So here's the deal — allowing "users" to work with computers they wanted to work with (including macs) is a great idea as most of the things you choose yourself is something you care more about than something chosen for you — but it also has the benefit of being flexible. You can get a good machine with a good spec now, and you don't have to take the slow standard one. Of course this creates some other topics of interest to the in-resident computer fixer. Antivirus is a must-have. But other than that (and basic computer skills which should be strived to be hired for) not much more is needed. You don't need to have everyone in the Windows azure ("domain") or be able to remote wipe users, etc. Because all other services are now in the cloud (files) you can still offboard users and safe guard files, just on another level. What if you need to reinstall? Reinstalling a windows or macOs-device is done super easy these days and not more a concern. Is the users not going to lose a lot of time by having to do all by themselves? I mean, you can still help them or guide them, but chances are that your see zero or no issues if you don't have an IT-problem issue ticket system for the employees, as they will attempt to fix it themselves and hello accountability. Knowing how to do the basics is really a basic skill these days. Antivirus software can be remotely managed via systems like Sophos and you can still watch over your users and be proactive. Do I have to mention that with so many employees working from home, it's also not practical to send someone "onsite" — and magically again the accountable employee will fix their issues themselves. For sensitive server based internal systems you could offer VPN – but really that is also slowing stuff down a bit. It depends. Really. Https encryption of traffic in your browser and using some kind of cloud tool is mostly enough today. As long as the network is protected, which peoples Wifi's today are and it's not too easy to hack 256-bit encryption. In fact it'll take all the time since the universe birth to brute force the password. Unless you have your cats name as wifi password.

The point is anyway that it's *enough*. If someone wanted to hack they could still do it, and you could anyway do nothing about it. Your systems is anyway in the cloud and sure the hacker could go thru your employees and social engineer access to their email accounts, then reset passwords and gain access to your systems, and copy data. But that is a training issue and may not be helped with higher security. Ransomware, when attackers encrypts the hard drive is "no real issue" as well, except loss of productivity as the files was saved to the cloud and backed up there, as opposed to how it was back in the days when everyone saved all on the desktop. Wait – you still do that?

When we are on the topic of basic IT Security – training and auditing training (where you test users via cases) is the way forward. The employees are the biggest security risk. So avoid sharing user accounts, always use named, use two-factor authentication (2FA) and use a smart password sharing tool like Bitwarden or LastPass. Often change shared passwords. Do not write passwords in the code (hello env files) but hey you already knew that. And yeah, if someone calls you and instruct you to say your password or pin – hang up...no one except a scammer will ever ever ask for that. Even in our MVP:ed SaaS systems we are building, customer agents can "log in as a user" instead of asking the customers for their password on the phone – right? And don't get me started on storing of credit card numbers.

LEADERSHIP

Lead developers, support them in their team building process, enable collaboration, empower and avoid micromanagement. But let's start with you.

CHAPTER 27

LEADING DEVELOPERS

Is working with developers and tech projects any different than leading people in other areas? Here we go thru topics such as leadership styles and basic ways of how to work with people in a way that is inspiring, motivating and is supporting people.

If you point one finger at someone else, three fingers are pointing back at yourself (Quote from unknown). Everything in leaderships starts with yourself.
– "If you can lead yourself you can lead others" (unknown).

When I lead basic agile leadership trainings at Maersk, I asked the participants to write down what they thought were great traits of leaders vs managers on a note. When presenting the results, traits for **managers** was such as "Divides work", "Reports to top management", "Has the budget", "Decides what we are going to do", "Sets the salary", "Tells me when I do something wrong" and "Is responsible for the work" and traits for **leaders** was such as (but very much not limited to) "Openness", "Fairness", "Should support me", "Takes decisions", "Listens to input", "Allows me to do what I'm good at", "Sees my potential", "Plans my career", "Approachable", "Has my back" and "Gives me feedback".

Everyone who aspires to be a leader, needs to take a good look in the proverbial mirror. What do you see? Why do you want to be a leader? Is it because you want the (usually) higher salary and feel better when you have more responsibility? Do you like working with people, and serving them and rake the gravel path in front of them?

In some companies feedback is given via a technique called 360. Colleagues, leaders and others who have been working with you will fill out a survey. HR gathers the results and presents a "picture" of you in a report. This is a very interesting concept from many angles.

First of all, you got to be calm and experience to handle your own feelings if you are going to be able to stomach what others think of you *for real* in a raw form. Handling feedback is not easy and may sometimes be seen as an attack on your own person. This is not the case. Feedback should always be "constructive" meaning suggest some improvements. Who gives feedback and how it's given will impact how you feel receiving it. Read more about feedback here.

Secondly, you may not recognise the feedback, as you may not be aware of what you are sending out. Imagine a square, upper left corner has "Open: Know to self and to other", upper right corner "Blind: Not known to self but known to others", bottom left corner: "Hidden: Known to self but not to others and bottom right corner: "Unknown: Not known to self or others". This model is called *Johari Window*. Making a 360 review may expose you to new things you didn't know from the Blind window. Some experience also points that being open about some things in Hidden may help others understand you better. Some teams "check in" in their morning meetings and start by saying what's on their minds like "my kid screamed the entire night so I slept bad" etc. This could help other understand how you behave in a certain way. Some people also consciously choose what to put in the Open window. It's how they want to be seen and perceived. It's very hard to keep a fake appearance up and some day it will crack, and expose the real person behind. Being more honest and open (by moving things from Hidden to Open) could help people being more authentic. The Blind corner could be that some people hears you clear your throat very loudly and you are not at all aware of it, or be a more deep issue like how you sneer, sigh or roll your eyes subconsciously when someone else is speaking. The Unknown window is a bit more new-agy as no one knows the things that's going on there. But you can learn new things about yourself.

Personality types

There are many personality tests out there and some may be better than others. It's indeed impossible to put people in boxes as we are a diverse breed where no one is like the other. But it's both interesting and helpful to draw some general patterns of personality types as they could be observed in a working environment. Let's list the most common personality types, at least in this theory.

Cool Blue

Great technicians, may respond more in a formal way and always have a deep knowledge of topics. Are not always sharing their opinion, because no one asked. Improves and makes things work. They invented atom bombs and space rockets.

Fiery Red

Purposed managers who know what they want and how to achieve it, running full speed ahead. Has no time to wait for others. Their greatest asset is fast thinking, which is also their greatest weakness. Will let everyone know their opinion, even if you didn't ask. These persons are creators, idea fountains and the ones making things happen.

Earth Green

Great team mates who listens and cares. Will deliver and are patient thru storms. Can be seen as slow, a bit boring, can be stubborn and reluctant to changes. Doers, fixes the admin behind others and makes the world tick.

Sunshine Yellow

Your office social animal who likes celebrations and a chance to discuss things. Can be a talk machine who loves their own voice. Brings in the engaging and inspiring aspect in to the work space.

Introvert — Thinking — Extrovert

GOOD DAY	BAD DAY	GOOD DAY	BAD DAY
Cautious	Stuffy	Competitive	Aggressive
Precise	Indecisive	Demanding	Controlling
Deliberate	Suspicious	Determined	Driving
Questioning	Cold	Strong-willed	Overbearing
Formal	Reserved	Purposeful	Intolerant
Cool Blue		**Fiery Red**	
GOOD DAY	BAD DAY	GOOD DAY	BAD DAY
Caring	Docile	Sociable	Excitable
Encouraging	Planned	Dynamic	Frantic
Sharing	Plodding	Demonstrative	Indiscreet
Patient	Reliant	Enthusiastic	Flamboyant
Relaxed	Stubborn	Persuasive	Hasty
Earth Green		**Sunshine Yellow**	

Feeling

Based on Analytical psychology theories founded by Carl Jung (1875 - 1961).

There are many depths and nuances into this with four letter combinations built on variations of NF (Intuition plus feeling, Earth Green), NT (intuition plus thinking, Cool Blue), SF (Sensing plus feeling, Sunshine Yellow) and ST (Sensing plus thinking, Fiery Red) directions in the Myers & Briggs Foundation theory which builds on Jung's theories.

It's a great idea to take a personality test. You can do it for free on a range of websites. 123-test has a free one on https://www.123test.com/jung-personality-test/. The report gives you some great insights built on generalisations, assumptions and observed behaviour of people who answered on the questions the same way like you did. So it's not really you.

Now that you have some great insights to how you most likely behave (or maybe you didn't agree at all) we can start applying these theories on the world around us. While you have been reading this text, I'm sure that you more or less subconsciously applied some of the personality descriptions to current or former colleagues. That's a fun exercise to do, even though we are talking about your experience here and in no way is that a representation of any universal "truths".

Let's jump straight in to it. As this is a book about working with developers and technical leadership, we will switch focus in to the actual developers. Who are they?

Developers

Software engineers, Full-stack developers, devs or whatever the title is, the human behind that is a normal person, believe it or not. They have the same need for safety in terms of a safe stress free working space, the need for feedback and appreciation as any other employee. There's no difference there.

What is different is that developers *mostly* have to figure out what they do and how they do it by themselves. This may sound weird, but as the technical landscape is moving in such a fast pace, no school could ever keep up to date with new trends or better solutions. Schools, programmes and courses can at best prepare developers with the basics, which is to understand software programming. Everything after that needs to be learned on the job.

Luckily there are tons of online sources for further learning, but the point is that this is not always clear to the developers themselves. You can say it's in the Unknown corner of the Johari Window. Junior (new) developers just staring a position are hungry and wants to try and does try to solve problems, by investing tons of time trying to find solutions on online forums. The more senior ones have experience and knows what's required of them, but even here they need to constantly evolve and learn new things, as the surrounding expects them to keep up to date and know many things.

Why is this interesting and how does it tie in to the lengthy chapter of personality types? Because developers are *usually* Fiery Red or Cool Blue types. And there you scroll up to remind yourself about these, as they became important. You check the column and see that Fiery Red are not at all Introverts. Why is not Earth Green a common type? (No one thought chatty Sunshine Yellows were common). There are many developers that may fall in to the Earth Green category, but in my experience it's not as common because of the point I made in that developers needs to constantly evolve. Earth Greens strive for stability and may not have the internal drive to handle the stress of the unknown, learning new things and constantly changing and evolving things. Fiery Reds will make whatever they need in order to make things happen; if learning React over a weekend will take them closer to their goals they will do it. They will never look back and care about things that was done, it's all about moving ahead. Some very successful developers are Fiery Red, which is interesting as they are seen as stressed and demanding individuals. But with strong drive comes great results. Usually at the cost of quality and a few colleagues stress level, but there you go.

Cool Blues is the most atypic and common personality trait working as a developer. They take their time to build something great, takes little or less input from others than formal documentation and will always remind Product people that it's important to do it right and follow certain coding standards. Cool Blues invented "Lint:ing" (ES Lint). That's a JavaScript analyse and fix engine which can find where in your code you do not have 4 spaces indented.

Some other very important parts to act on here is how Fiery Reds and Cool Blues would like to have their internal communication received. How they would like to participate in meetings. Here's a big difference as many Sunshine Yellows thrive and get a lot of energy from meetings and interactions with other human beings (the definition of extrovert). The Fiery Reds would like to participate in meetings so *they* can talk themselves and tell people what's going to happen, as they have already moved on in their heads. Earth Greens would like to see how everyone else is doing and have a good talk. Cool Blues may want to be in the meeting, as long as the topic is a technical one. There should be time to thoroughly discuss the depths of the issue and there should be no rush in to decisions. So if the meeting is a quick (Red) "let's do this, let's go"-meeting, the Cool Blues are not going to say anything. Their analysis minds is both waiting to be asked for their opinion, at the same time dreading to have to explain the most simplest things to people who doesn't get it.

So when planning meetings with developers, make sure to know your team, or you will get to know them fast. "All hands" meetings will very rarely be productive, unless it's facilitated by a very strong leader who can keep the meeting on the track and at the same time hold off the pushy Reds.

Developers not only needed to learn most of their jobs on the job, but also needed to handle a working situation which was "unclear", to say the least. If they joined early in the company they needed to handle uncertainty and try to bring order in to the chaotic requests, ideas and demands that others were giving them. Try to create business logic from a bran storming meeting! Going from vision to a coded application requires a lot of trial and error, agile working approaches and patience.

A developer normally choose their job because it was to do with computers, was something that they could create using their own skills. Coming from the schools, they never had any idea that they also had to manage multiple stakeholders and be in so many meetings.

This is important because developers will, as much as they can, avoid meetings and have a preference for working on their own. That's why many developers were already working from home a long time before the Covid-19 pandemic hit and everyone was forced to adapt. Developers slowly started to get permission from their managers to work from home. As results increased, it was slowly extended. If you walk in to an office today, and actually find developers in some corner, they will most likely sit with earphones on listening to their music, and write to each other over Slack. I'm mentioning this here as it goes in to their basic needs. Of course there are developers that like other people and doesn't have any problem working in open office spaces, but most does not.

Imagine that you have to read something really really thorough and find spelling mistakes. This is almost important to do in an open office environment where the Sales person (sorry, I mean Key Account Managers) talks loud on the phone or the happy chatty office person is engaged in an intense conversation about the next summer party, involving everyone in the office wether they like it or not. This is not working for developers.

The next job that developer got, they demanded to work from home, "remote". As developers are a very thought out and wanted group of talent, it became less and less possible for companies to hire them unless they accepted this.

Giving developers their own space, a lot of time to code and only meetings where it makes sense, means giving them what they need in order to do their job.

Having zero meetings is also not the solution at all. As a leader, one needs to establish a healthy meeting culture where people can get involved on their terms.

Consider communication with developers on their terms, via Slack/Teams instead of suggesting in person or online face-to-face meetings. At the same time, as many things can get lost in text messaging, it's important to keep meeting face-to-face.

Developers are humans though, as everyone else they have needs and gets motivated in similar way as others.

Facilitate

As a leader you should invest in people – meaning – be interested in people; how they are feeling, what they do and what makes them tick. Support and help them succeed and you will both learn and achieve a lot. As a leader you are the facilitator, who's responsible to help and support the team. A so called "servant leader". This doesn't mean you can't set high expectations and work to build a high performing team in this way. But go away from the old command and control-mindset that was so popular back in the days.

When building a team

So you know who you are and how you react in different situation, you know the typical developer traits. Now you can start building your team. The first thing to look out for, is to **not** have everyone being the same type. Sure, it's the easy way to hire a certain type of people (even that is impossible though). But do you really want a team that only codes and never discusses or have any conflicts? That never comes up with solutions no one ever could think of, *because* they discussed and disagreed? Having a diverse team means more work for you, but also better outcomes.

To build a high-performing team there are a few base ingredients to put in to the mix. Number one is the hardest to do for many leaders. It's to **stop managing**. As per the Agile manifest the best teams are self-organised. They can handle it, as they are adults. Read more about team dynamics in the Forming Chapter.

Accountability

The most important ingredient in all collaboration is Accountability and Self-leadership. It's everyones responsibility to:

Say you'll do something and actually do it

Committing to do something on time and letting people know ahead of time if you are going to miss the due date

Letting others know when there is a problem or you need help, instead of creating a crisis for everyone

Not blaming others (teammates, other departments, or family members) when things go wrong

Not voicing complains (repeatedly) without offering or participating in finding solutions

Not being the naysayer when changes are discussed and resist anything new

Not focusing on your personal success at the expense or exclusion of others

Not settling for mediocrity in your performance, teamwork or communication

Apologize and take ownership when you make a mistake, and learn from it as well

Not expecting to be rewarded or promoted just for showing up to work without demonstrating high performance, or thinking you're the best when you aren't

Content from the book "Making yourself indispensable: the power of personal accountability" (Mark Samuel, 2012)

CHAPTER 28

FORMING

When a new team gets together, there are certain dynamics at work. Understanding these basics helps you understand what's going on.

You have managed to get the entire team to that team offsite. The trip in went well and everyone have arrived. It's time to present the new team members to each other. The meeting room has the classic chairs around a table. You talk, present goals and give your intro. The team members are silent. No one has any questions. Breaking for lunch, it's slowly taking off with some easier discussions among the team about hobbies and fishing stories. Going back to the meeting room and the teams seems more at easy. But not everyone seems to be interested. Some are starting to participate (and talk) more than others. Already day two you can see people clustering in smaller groups, finding their favourites. When one is going, others are following.

This is the first step in the FIRO (Fundamental Interpersonal Relations Orientation) circle of team forming. Another famous one is called "Forming, Norming, Storming, Performing". We'll touch on a slightly modified FIRO here.

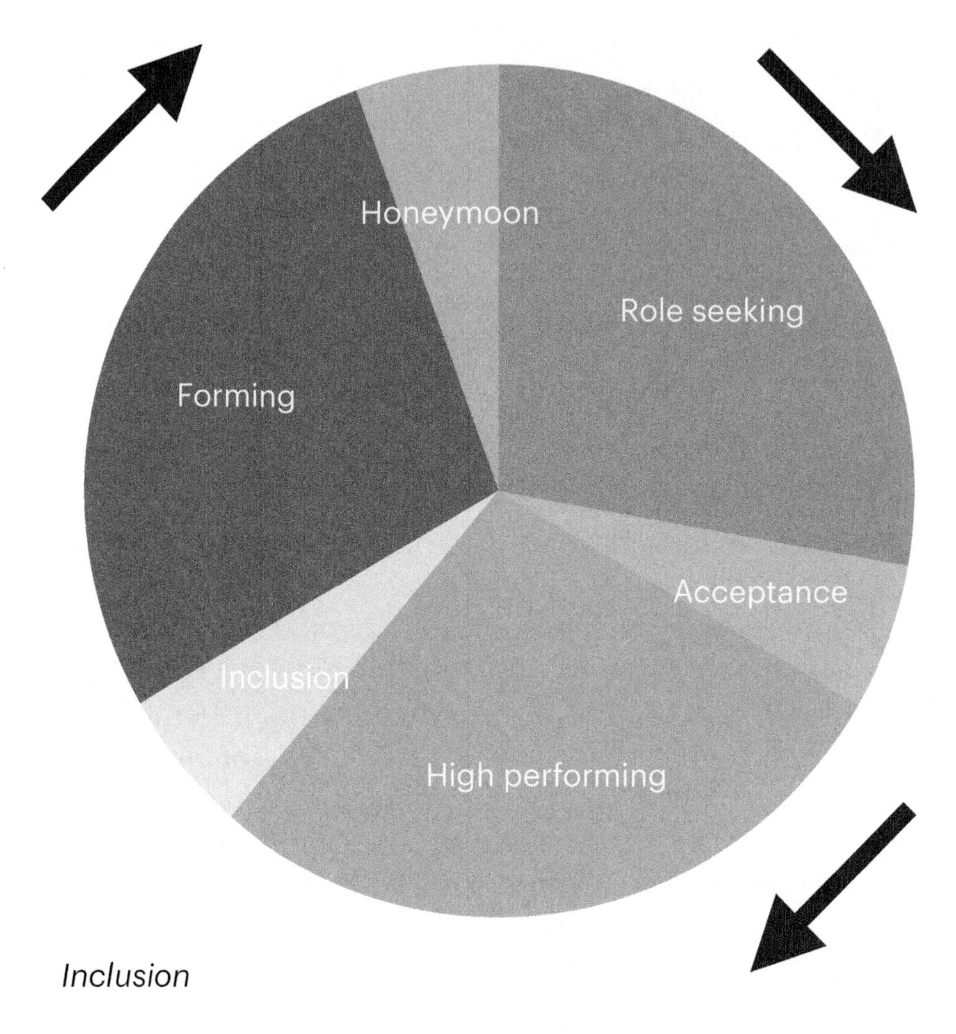

Inclusion

The first step is for team members to actively decide if they want to be a part of this team. They are sitting in the boat and wonder if they want to join.

Forming

The team gets together and getting to know each other. The topics are not very loaded. No one wants to take too much space and people are seeking to see how others react when one is speaking, how is it received and what's the effect.

Honeymoon

The team has done forming and are working well together. It can feel like you are a part of the best team ever and that it's really great to be here. Like a honey moon. People are helping each other, displaying patience, not taking too much space and sharing tasks and letting everyone talk.

Role seeking

The honeymoon is over. Now the role seeking phase is going in to stormy times. Team members are increasingly challenging each other and questioning openly. Conflicts, arguments, back stabbings – it's all here. Participants clusters in smaller groups and are undermining others. It can be heated sometimes.

Acceptance

The team moves to this phase only when they are done role seeking and sadly not all the teams makes it. There needs to be a sufficient level of feedback, acceptance and "agree to disagree". Conflicts will need to be "resolved" or at least overcome so they are not hindering work.

High performing

If, and only if, the team managed, with the help from their servant leader, to move passed the Role seeking phase, accepted each other – then they can begin work as a high performing team. Being in a high performing team feels almost like the Honeymoon phase. It's great but it doesn't come without a lot of work. The air is cleared from the big conflict. It's like on a warm humid summer day when the rain comes in and clears the air – it leaves a fresh and crisp feeling.

Supporting the team in the phases

As a leader, you need to facilitate the team thru the different phases so they can move on. But at the same time, they need to have the experience. No one can be high performing from day 1.

During the first phases it's important to give a good introduction and give a feeling of the company culture, making it easier for the team members themselves to want to join in mentally.

Having clear roles and responsibilities, expecting a high standard when it comes to behaviour and respect as well as demanding team members to take show a high level of self-leadership is going to be imperative for a successful time thru the Role seeking phase. If you as a leader have been vague on responsibilities you will for sure have people fighting over who's going to do what. As a leader, you need to be strong in this phase and be very clear. Facilitating conflicts – and never ever let people hide those conflicts under the carpet. The worst thing is when one team member goes to the "boss" and give negative feedback about another team member, and the boss takes the feedback further personally. That's not ok and a very common trap. Conflicts between individuals needs to be resolved between individuals. It may need to be facilitated, but taking someone else's story as your own is not going to help the conflict to be solved. It's also very threatening for a team member to hear this from their leader, as if they agree. Then it becomes a truth, even if it was just an experience from just one person. If team members are making themselves spokes persons by saying "I think I speak for everyone by saying..." doesn't work. Feedback can only come from one person to another person and only reflects their own experience. Any "packaging" from a self imposed mini-manager must be shut down immediately.

Once (and if) the team reaches the High performing phase they don't need their leader for much. Formally approving company budgets, facilitating contacts with the rest of the organisation and giving them space to breath is still needed and should be on top of the priority list for any great leaders.

What can disturb the paradise

When existing team members leaves, the team can go in to the Role seeking phase again or sometimes even as far back as to the Inclusion. The great leader needs to pick up on this and facilitate discussions, listen to the team members and help out where needed. If a new team member is joining, this can also trigger a teams move back in the FIRO circle. A team that has been in the High performing phase knows how it feels and will want to get back to it, so they will help the process to get there again. This means both trying to fill the gap or voice what's needed to fill the gap of the departing team member, and be highly involved in making it happen. They will buddy up with new team members and help them get up to speed quickly.

Having the team self-organise may be slightly more storming than if you'd direct and tell everyone what to do, but the benefits is that the team will come to a completely different level and achieve much more than under your control. Don't be that micro manager.

The commitment

It's also worth mentioning that every person joining a team must make a commitment. They must commit to respect, be honest, treat everyone equally and to be a part of the team. If the company culture is a disrespectful and toxic one where managers are screaming to their employees or treating people different because of gender or origin, you are not likely to get anyone in their right mind to join the company. At the same time the team member must make this commitment, and stick to it thru the hard times and the good. This demands people to show accountability. Then good things will come.

CHAPTER 29

COLLABORATION MODELS

Let's visit some interesting collaboration models and how they have been working out.

Spotify are famous among developer circles for their collaboration model. At the time it came, it was something new and fresh. Built on agile principles but also having a bigger company performance in mind. The model, which is about scaling scrum, also takes the entire team structure and collaboration in to account. Other popular models are LeSS, the among agile practitioners hated SAFe and Teal.

I have chosen to look at these models specifically as it makes sense when working with developers. There are many other bigger models that's on an organisational level but let's stay in scope here.

The Spotify Model

Invented by Spotify, the Spotify model completely changed the way development teams were working. Even the ones not a part of Spotify. Videos and great examples was shared showing how fund and interesting things were at Spotify. Being so early with this way of collaborating, they set a standard in the industry.

The Spotify model is in a way a scaled version of scrum. It focuses on team autonomy and self-organisation. It relies on people to reach objectives and achieve goals.

Working at Spotify you are a part of a Tribe. People are divided in to Squads which each has a Product Owner. Horizontally team members of the Squads are also a part of a Chapter.

The cross-functional Squad can be compared to an agile team and consists of 6 to 12 people who are autonomously responsible for a certain feature area of the Product. They have their own road map, Product Owner with a product vision and who assigns priorities. They are supported by an agile coach. The work they do is as much a possible with so little dependencies on other outside team as possible. The Squads chose their own agile methodology (Kanban, Scrum etc).

Chapters are groups where team members can join and discuss certain topics such as best practices and architecture. This is the backbone that holds the squads together.

Guilds can include team members from across the entire company and their scope is broader.

LeSS

Large-Scale Scrum is a popular model to build on the benefits of working in an agile scrum environment. Basically there are multiple streams of scrums happening at the same time, with multiple ScrumMasters and participants building increments to a product.

LeSS have a structure of Feature teams and communities to discuss best practices and share experience.

SAFe

Scaled-Agile Framework popped up when large companies were confused between the difference of Digital Transformation and Agile Transformation. SAFe stepped in and offered a model which can be scaled on an organisational level. It's a wide framework with rules and systems for everything from Organisational Agility, Lean Portfolio Management, Agile Product Delivery, Team and Technical Agility to Continuous Learning Culture.

It has been criticised by agile evangelists that it's a fake agile framework, called "Scrumfall". True agile should be easy to understand and overview, and not be determined beforehand. At least in an Agile transformation, the employee needs to go thru their own transformation and Agile "aha" – and implementing SAFe may jump this important step. Many parts of SAFe is indeed not agile at all, which the trained eye can see looking at their process map.

However having some agile methods may be better than none.

Teal

Invented by Frederic Laloux 2014, and based on years of research, Teal is a way to organise companies which is characterised by self-management, wholeness and a deeper sense of purpose. Forget organisational charts hierarchies or even goals. A teal organisation has self-managed teams which are lead by intuitive reasoning and decentralised decision-making.

Teal is seen as the fifth stage of evolve meant of organisations.

Red (impulsive)

Imagine the first step in which authority is enforced using power. Like street gangs and mafia.

Breakthroughs: Division of labor, top-down authority.

Amber (conformist)

A disciplined organisation built on beliefs common to the group where shame and guilt is used to enforce authority. Like in the church and the army.

Breakthroughs: Replicable processes, a stable organization chart.

Orange (achievement)

The world is a predictable machine and can be controlled to achieve a certain outcome. A scientific approach. Like Wall Street banks and some startups.

Breakthroughs: Innovation, accountability, meritocracy.

Green (pluralistic)

An organisation which has a higher level inclusion and strives to treat everyone as equal. Can be similar to that being in a family. Popular in non-profit and non-government organisations.

Breakthroughs: Empowerment, values-driven culture, stakeholder value.

Teal (evolutionary)

The fifth step is Teal, where everyone listens to their inner voice. They drop their "mask" and join fully in their mind, and not only what is seen as "professional". Everyone contributes based on their unique potential.

Breakthroughs: Self-management, wholeness, evolutionary purpose.

Is teal the next stage of how we work in the future? Where private life (or "private" feelings) and job has merged together and we achieve a higher purpose? Are we to be guided by our inner voice, the gut feeling to make better decisions and reach better outcomes? At the first sight it may seem as a somewhat big bite to chew. But in the rest of our lives, those hours outside work – do you have quarterly goals, a career plan and report to someone for all the decisions you take? Can you go fully in to an organisation in mind and life, driven by your purpose?

Teal Source: What is a Teal Organization? https://workology.com/what-is-a-teal-organization/ (Monica Giannobile, 2022)

CHAPTER 30

WORKING REMOTE

The last two years has proven that "work from home" is here to stay, and is already the default way of working in the future.

Home office, as it was called before, has been around for a long time. At least for developers it was great to be able to stay home, feed the cat and get to develop undisturbed for a few hours a week. It was always seen as a "perk" and was more excused as "the plumber is coming" or "I'll be getting a delivery" so one needed to stay home to open the door. Some developers were already working as "coding nomads" and there were even companies offering only remote work, but it was kind of frowned upon from others.

Along came the Covid-19 pandemic with shut down offices and home office as a result. All of a sudden employees were supposed to solve their home working situation, with or without screaming kids or loud spouses, with little or zero help from the formerly purposeful HR-departments. Most companies saw this as a way to survive the pandemic and employees did what they could to accommodate. Fast forward two years and we have a situation where most people don’t really want to "go back to the office”. It's very individual and takes up many dinner conversations. Some really like the office and the small talk, the quick chats and the option to fast interact with peers. Some others have built new lives during these years and filled the 2-4 hours commute a day with other purposeful activities such as being able to eat breakfast with their children without stress, or walk them to day care. Some others just slept longer and woke up rested and more balanced, instead of having to steal a quick nap between the train changes.

Many companies have adapted to this new way of working, because it was actually much more efficient. Go in to any “dev floor” (if you find any) where developers are still working side by side and guess what — they all have earphones and communicate with each other using Slack. Some companies are launching campaigns to get "their" employees" back. Why, one may wonder.

■■

What home office / remote work can never do is to replace a meeting in person. It's still the strongest way of collaborating between humans, and we say a lot with our body language than with a few lines of text using Slack or with video. However it’s not always the most efficient way of communicating. Some argues the hybrid model where you have set days in the office and set days working from home could work better. I think the best way of handling it is to let the teams decide for themselves. This is a bit scary for managers who's sole role is to "manage" people and control output. Luckily, there are fewer and fewer of these managers left out there, but they do still exist. They are right now going thru an existential threat to their roles. What should they do now if they have no people to follow up on next to them or chase people for updates? It's really a big problem for those who didn't switch into leading teams. Managers are a die hard breed. Are all managers bad? No, not at all. Many things needs to be managed: Websites, Patches of servers. But not people. They are fully able to self-manage. They went thru school, applied to jobs, managed life-juggling, pays their bills, got the drivers license and manages to procrastinate as little as possible. Or do they not? So there is really no need to have Managers at all. Having Managers around creates *management* which is far from the same as leadership. It's another die hard leftover from the Industrial era. Let it die with the Covid-19 pandemic.

When the winds of change are blowing, some people build wind shelters — others wind mills. Many are those who transformed from being Managers to Leaders, with great success. Leaders are followed, respected — and to one extent awed. Managers are usually just "listened to" or "accepted" in the best case, or in the worst just a reason to leave the company.

Why is the topic of Managers important to remote work? Because when working remotely, you *must* self-manage. And most people who end up in a new role, will adapt and deliver. The alternative is chaos and out of that there will be order.

Being a leader leading remote teams you can still do tons of things to engage and motivate your team. Offsite meetings, remote meetings with break-out topics, online discussions, breakfast meetings in person, breakfast meetings not in person, order pizzas to everyone at home and eat together, play online games, have a hackathon tournament, travel around and meet your team at their favourite coffee place, keep people in the loop on Slack, involve, delegate responsibility. Create a "pull" not a "push" for meetings, by making them interesting and non-mandatory. Some argues being a leader is harder and maybe it is. But the respect you get as a leader and the respect you feel from the teams are well worth the effort versus "telling". So go out there and lead by example!

Adjusting to a remote working environment also allows for low office costs but also helps you tap in the ever growing international talent pool — you can have developers working in many different countries, covering time zones and delivering stuff while you are sleeping.

Some Managers argues there is less control and you have no idea what the developers are doing. Well, you can still be a micro manager by checking git checkout logs, access logs, contribution rates, Jira throughput an other useless ways of controlling people. I think it's better to trust people to do their job and to be available to support if they need any help — with the code, with the task or if they simply need someone to discuss with.

Trust people and amazing things will happen.

CHAPTER 31

AVOIDING MICRO MANAGEMENT

The biggest threat to self-managed employees who would like to get a higher sense of inclusion and has an inner drive.

Accountability is an interesting word. It means "the fact or condition of being accountable; responsibility". Google says that: "lack of accountability has corroded public respect for business and political leaders". I will get back to why Accountability is the remedy against micro management. But first, a little story.

Meet Johnny and Elsa. Both are new to the company and their teams. Johnny has been hired as a Manager and Elsa as an "Individual contributor". Johnny takes on his new role with great vigour. He interviews his team members, get's to know them by first name and ask for their strengths. Team members listens carefully to their new manager (perhaps because they are afraid to lose their jobs?). It's also important to make an impression so when Johnny makes a half-hearted joke, some chuckle semi-fake or tries to laugh supportively. Johnny sets out to go thru his task list and implement the changes he sees fit with a strong drive. He is the manager.

Elsa is also new to the team, but she is more careful in team meetings. She want's to feel the waters a bit before she speaks up. What if she says the wrong things? Her team members are nice to her and listens, but sometimes a bit more passively. They hope she wont question the status quo too much. Any challenge from her at this point would be fended off or ignored.

What's the difference here? A piece of paper saying who has what role. The rest is self invented by Johnny and Elsa. What says that Elsa can't sit down one-to-one with her new team colleagues and get to know them? Nothing is limiting her from doing that. The only difference between Johnny and Elsa are that piece of paper, probably a salary level and the act. Nothing else. So what is stopping people from taking this step? Why do we do it just because we are told so?

■■

What if we all could just take on our job with a feeling of ownership and full accountability? We could actually – and some people are doing just that, in their own way. But, along comes **micro managers** and destroys the party.

Demanding to know the details, changing priorities, debating the nitty-gritty, moving around things, adjusting text and approving others work the micro managers are perhaps the biggest cost for a company these days. Aiming for perfection, they steal the happiness, work quality, efficiency and proudness from the employees work. Creating drones that will only do a part, only to get it changed. Not daring to take accountability as it's constantly shot down by the micro manager. Hiding behind words like "quality" and "I must approve" they slowly take away the motivation and creativity from the employees. Demanding to have it their way they stop process, holding of progress, stamping on collaboration and the most important — is killing accountability.

If you give out a task or delegate a problem to someone — do not expect the solution to be exactly like you want it yourself. If you think like this — you are a micro manager. Delegation means losing control. Taking a step back is very hard and requires a lot of leadership skills and self preservation. In return though, you'll create self driven co-workers who will constantly over-deliver and drive things they way they want it — and that my friends is a huge motivational source. Being motivated leads to happiness. Happy people performs better over long time. This is the complete opposite to stress.

Leading big teams efficiently spells Accountability, either to a few people or jointly to the entire team. Give them the budget! They will do everything they can to deliver against it. Nothing is as rewarding as being able to control your own work. And there you are as their leader, supporting them and cheer them on from the side.

There is no need to parent, tell, punish or micro manage your employees. In the vacuum that your stepping back is creating, new self-driven leaders will form and they will cover the gaps and deliver something probably much better than if you would have micro managed it.

Most books on this topic tend to be high level. I want to be super detailed about what micro management is and how it's perceived, by a few stories. Here we go:

You ask an employee to change the new customer Welcome Letter. The employee is excited and sets out to do their best. They deliver back a new text. You review it and find small errors, suggest new texts and sentences as well as questioning the ugly design. The employee understands your feedback (it's now *their* letter and they are automatically responsible for how ugly it was before and now needs to fix it). The employee slowly learns how you think and focus on delivering a solution to *you*, slowly stopping to think themselves. After a few more rounds of reviews and error finding, you approve the work and it can be used. The employee has no feeling of being able to create something, there is no joy, it's just "done". Meanwhile you probably also found some other tasks that were urgent and since this was not longer on *your* priority list, it's no longer important. The employee keeps getting tasks from you and continues to try to "deliver" to what they think you want instead of doing what they think the customer wants (what they were probably hired for). So instead of a contributor they are now your tool, in fact just someone to execute what you slowly fool yourself is something great.

This is **micro management**. The process takes a long time and meanwhile the old ugly letter is still out there, and your so-called "feedback" is doing more harm than good.

You ask an employee to change the text of the Welcome Letter, but instead of giving clear instructions of what to change you ask them to use their experience, their own thoughts to come up with a solution on their own. Then they come back asking for a review you say: "I don't need to approve it, I trust you it's great as you usually do great stuff".

The employee will still find some peers to get feedback from but showing you trust the employee to run with it themselves, you are also creating an environment which enables Accountability. Employees will take a much higher interest, set their own high quality goals and challenge themselves and others to a higher degree rather than trying to deliver to their manager. And seeing the impact of how the Welcome Letter is received by your customers the employees feel proud and motivated. They know they made a difference. They saw something from idea to done.

Which type of employees do you want to work with? The drones doing what they are told, with a deteriorating motivation or the super charged accountable ones you can trust to bridge gaps when they see them?

CHAPTER 32

MOTIVATION

Culture eats Strategy for breakfast

Before even touching the topic of motivation, I'd like to talk about some very important prerequisites I think needs to be there. Trying to motivate people without having great leaders is like try to make a Volvo 240 from 1982 balance on their back wheels only. It's impossible. So as with so many other things, we need to clean our own entrance first as the Swedish saying goes.

A great thing to start with is to have great leaders, open people and a welcoming culture. Easier said than done, and this is of course not easy to have. Didn't say that. But it's also very hard to build on the motivation of people unless you have the above. Some people are self-motivated by the new feeling about changing their role and starting in a new company, getting to know new people and are busy learning their new job. But long term, they'll slowly get unmotivated unless they receive feedback and are encouraged. In 2016 I wrote an MBA Master Thesis about "What motivates professional early millennials in the workplace and what is the best way to manage them to reach their potential?". Spoiler alert, it turns out that it has very little do with the actual age.

I did identify these 5 areas. And this is actual research, built on personal interviews qualitative interviews.

#1: Give feedback

Millennials, and generation X for that sake, seek to understand how well they are performing and if they meet the expectations, and adjusts to the feedback. Feedback is the single most important motivator. Make sure that feedback is honest, based on observable behaviour and is actionable. Feedback is not always received well and it would be advisable that managers who are supposed to give feedback learns about the technique in order to both understand the concept but also be prepared to deal with outcomes.

#2: Share responsibilities

Enable employees to grow by giving them a great deal of responsibility. They will grow with it. Challenging tasks, still manageable and not too overwhelming in an area of potential growth would be advisable. Some people will handle "deep-water" and a "sink-or-swim" environment but most employees will be set out for failure. It's advisable to support and mentor the employee, without micro-managing or being intrusive.

#3: Offer flexibility

Enable employees to make their own schedules that fits with their work. Never micro-manage time or have a 9am to

5pm schedule where everyone must show up, if possible. Offer remote options, as long as it fits the job. Offer flexibility also in the way the work is performed. Less stringent processes bed to creativity, and with creativity innovation is at least enabled.

#4: Reward

Recognise good efforts and reward with praise and company wide recognition. This also includes monetary bonus when needed however employees are motivated higher by compassion and good working conditions.

#5: Support

Make sure the best managers are hired that cares about people first of all. Managers that doesn't manage, but coaches and helps bring out the best of the employees. Support employees in their challenging work situations but never take over.

Further, to be honest about career options and to offer trainings that supports this is perceived as good but it's not highest on the list of what motivates millennials.

If the topic of motivation interests you, you can read much more on my blog https://robert.mejlero.com/5-things-to-motivate-millenials-to-reach-their-full-potential/ and download the full thesis in all eBook formats for free here: https://robert.mejlero.com/master-thesis-what-motivates-early-millennials-in-the-workplace/

Does it disturb you that these topic is concerning "millennials"? By 2025 it's estimated that 75% of the workforce are millennials.

The topic of motivation is much bigger than what can be covered here.

CHAPTER 33

INNOVATION

An innovation process. An oxymoron.

On one axis you have innovation, the other side process. They are their own complete opposites. There is no innovation in a process. It follows its steps, any attempt to bypass, go outside the box or follow another path and the process stops. Doesn't compute. There is no place whatsoever for wiggle room, suggestions, changes, other approaches or innovation. The process goes forward in its established way. Of course you can change the process, and believe it or not but most business projects is about making a process easier/more efficient and is the entire base of huge projects. So there can indeed be innovation in the *change work* of processes. Innovation – if I may interpret it as "they way to think freely without borders and create ideas or concepts that are not necessarily done before or grounded in reality". To have an innovative process we need a creative environment. Sure, some people just gets an idea when they have seen a certain system long enough or identified a problem — and if they are heard and listened to some great things can indeed happen. Life found its way thru multiple random events, it's believed.

For a long time I thought that you can't do this. You can't put people in a room and ask them to create. But it is possible, and really not that hard. What's hard is, again, the prerequisites.

Take people out of their normal comfort zone. Put them in an environment where they don't have to impress their boss or despise their colleagues. Present a group with a challenge. Ask them to work together. Ask them to create solutions. They will do it. It will be crazy ideas and as the newly founded team is also going thru their classic forming-norming-storming-performing process as all teams to in the beginning, they may not work "efficiently" or even involve everyone in the team. Some "natural" leaders will take over and force others to build their idea. But given time, they will at least come to the norming stage.

This is a standard way of looking at problems and thinking up solutions. Nothing bad. What amazed me that innovation could come out of conflict and feedback.

Put some other teams of a different challenge. They should now review the ideas from team 1 and come with improvements. Then present this to them. By doing this, you are overlapping skills and the end product will be much better. Try it. The worst thing you can have in a team is "yes sayers" who just does what they are told. So this is how you setup an innovation process. Get the ideas scrutinised, by other "free" teams that doesn't act out of an agenda. This is a way of gathering feedback. It may not be what the innovators want to hear and feedback is a beast, that's for sure. But it's valuable.

■■

Fostering and enabling innovation comes mostly out of having the basics: culture, empowerment, self-managed and autonomous diverse teams. If people dare to be themselves, speak up, suggest and run with their ideas – they will not just "do their job". Instead they will continuously improve the product all day every day as that's what real innovation is about. Daring to question, ask they why and then act. Test. Get feedback. Do again.

An easy way to stamp down and suppress innovation is to micro manage. Do that by asking for something, then critically review what you get back, ask for changes based on your own feelings and ideas, ridicule the result, ignore the experts around you with real experience, say that you know best, call people idiots. And then blame others that they are not innovative.

CHAPTER 34

FEEDBACK

They beauty of working with others is that they experience things about you. And users experience a lot using your product.

What's harder in life than hearing something you have been working on or been a part of is not working to another persons expectations or that someone you've worked with, delivered a product to or collaborated with has had a really bad experience? Feedback can and is a real mental exercise unlike anything else. If you let it.

There are tons of angles in to feedback and I will try to generalise about a combination of common denominators for feedback from users of your products, "bosses" and colleagues. I'm not going to touch your laundry room conflicts though. Even though someone should.

■■

Personal Feedback

First, let's dig into how feedback arises. It arises from an experience. It's and individual experience that someone has interacting with something. It doesn't mean that "everyone" would have the same experience, or that they wouldn't either for that matter. But any attempt from a person having said experience and says "I think I speak for everyone when I say that" needs to be closed down quick. People can only speak about their own experience from their own perspective and those who tries to be spoke persons shouldn't trouble theirselves.

An experience comes from a way that a person perceives their surroundings, their own past experiences, their ability to feel compassion and empathy with others as well as their mindset. There are probably tons of more stuff that can be said here, but the point is that you, who would be receiving the feedback, should see the perspective they are offering.

With this perspective, it's perhaps easier to listen to the feedback. From my perspective, it's not needed to agree or change everything you do because someone had a certain experience with you. It's up to you. That's why they say that feedback is a gift. There's these "feedback ladders" with different steps of how to handle feedback with first rejection, then ignore, then listen, later understanding the need for change and last doing something about it (act) but again we are hitting the scope roof of this book. Key takeaway is that not all feedback are bad and not all are good either.

Feedback from a manager is standard. Too many times though they speak from an agenda that they think some areas of your personality needs change or that some tasks could have been better done or gotten more attention (again their perspective) so they colour their feedback with their own ideas of who you should be. Take what makes sense for you (what you didn't see or knew someone could experience about you) and throw away the rest in a deep trash bin somewhere. Too much here is fake to be useful. Unless you keep hearing the same thing from many different people, at in that point you probably would want to see if you could do something about it. In that case actually doing something about it could improve situations for yourself. Don't change because someone else wants you too. Change because you want it yourself. Enough of Dr. Phil here.

So let's rush in to user feedback. In many ways totally different from feedback from your boss or a colleague, but it does also come from that said experience someone had with, not you, but your product.

Conflicts

I also want to touch the topic of conflicts. Most people don't like them. I think that's a fair assumption to make. But it all depends I guess. Some say the best teams delivers the best results when they have had a conflict, resolved it together and moved on, despite their differences. Conflict is whether we like it or not a big piece of working together. Most talk behind backs that some people do is built on that they don't understand each other. Look at that! I just solved the biggest problem in the world. Anyhow, don't do the mistake of trying to solve the conflict on behalf of people. Instead encourage them to solve it themselves without your involvement. If that doesn't work, HR can help out. Don't dodge it or sweep it under the rug though. Some great leaders embraces the conflict and addresses the "elephant in the room" which clears the air.

If conflicts are left unresolved, they are most likely to go off at a later stage and will be be able to be contained anymore. The longer you wait to address it, the bigger the boom later. Waiting out conflicts will not make them go away. What happens instead is that it grows larger and can spin out of control. It could even lead to physical violence or people quitting their jobs.

User Feedback

User feedback is the bread and water and what can light the fire of Product development! If we don't get it we know nothing. Nada. Zip. Zero. How do we know what features to develop and how they are used? We don't. Otherwise we would make our best bet, based on what our managers pushed thru with. Where we should make our best with our best ideas of how we think the user behaves based on our experiences. In some cases data, yes. But for the testing and to see what works, gathering feedback is crucial. User feedback is not only listening to the very few people who actually decided to contact you and voice their concerns or needs. It's a part, sure, and one that can be listened and acted on if it makes sense. Using this source only to build your Product on is a serious mistake. So let's take the example that a customer calls in to customer support and says they can't find the login button and don't understand how it works to login. Is that your Products fault? I mean there are maybe a certain base level of understanding that needs be there by the users. Maybe your Product can be the first to solve this, but most likely not. So moving around the Login-button or make the login fields bigger may solve the problem or make it slightly better for the angry customer who didn't get it – but it will not make it better for those other customers who didn't call in or had any problems with this. In fact, acting on feedback from one type of customer only and not taking time to seek feedback from others may result in that you are making it a lot worse instead. Who to listen to is a big topic, but a simple profitability analysis can help you. See who actually contributes most to the bottom line (money earned). It can though go wrong, in that things are complex and not so easy. But it's better than guessing.

The worst source of feedback is managers who didn't try the application themselves or relayed feedback from others like their mom or any other close relative. Or just had an angry customer on the phone and now wants to "solve the problem" asap. It can make you take a completely wrong turn and start building and optimising for a group that is never going to make your Product profitable. So choose your feedback source wisely.

The most valuable source of feedback is not how users or co-workers experienced your product when they clicked around, oh no. The better source is their interactions, events — what they actually did and what was used and how. Hello data. It feels sad that this huge topic, which shows how users voted by clicking only gets a few lines of attention, but it's where you can extrapolate, learn, see results in an unbiased data driven way. Without data you are just another person with an opinion.

CHAPTER 35

TIME OFF

Do you want to spend time approving leave requests?

Let everyone decide their own working time, when to take time off and how to manage and handle their own work. Again, we are dealing with adults who took themselves thru schools, activities, exams and probably even got kids and manages all that without any problem. Your best bet is to treat people like adults and let them manage this themselves.

What is important, is that it's communicated. I keep an "absence calendar" shared where everyone can just put in when they are out. It's easy for everyone to see and no one needs to ask around where people are.

For the employee they also need to step up and make it work around their time and work load. Nothing is wrong with saying no or asking for more time. The worst is over-promising and under-delivering. Everything can happen, but keeping the ones you work with informed about when you are available or not, is a good thing to do and it'll help avoid a lot of confusion.

Letting people take care of this themselves also free's up a lot of time. All of a sudden no one needs "approvals" to go to the doctor, so basically people will also be more motivated.

■■

Some companies have a free vacation policy. Meaning they can take as much vacation as they want to. Some has put a bit of a restrain on it and set like "what's good for you is good for us" and "manage with responsibility". I have heard of some good examples when this worked really good (Danske Banks former innovation hub in Copenhagen, Denmark) — and I think it's an interesting concept. Just as long as it doesn't force people to check in more and work more I guess it's a great thing. People need to breathe.

My take on this is more micro though. Why not take a break in the middle of the day, go for a run or do your favourite activity for 1-2 hours combined with a lunch – and you can return fresh for the afternoon shift. In this way you can always keep yourself in motion and that's great for the endorphins and the self-esteem. And you get a little break during the day to recharge. A quick recharge perhaps but whatever works to relieve stress and pressure is good. Too many people over-work and try to achieve stuff on their own or tries to deliver to the ever demanding micro managing boss who has no respect that you may have other things on your plate and needs their stuff "now now now". Even that pressure can be relieved by blocking out 2 hours of your calendar during the day where you can do whatever you want. Just read up on the news, watch the rain, go for a walk or anything else. In the evenings it's harder, when the family comes home and it's full on again.

Many people moved up to the mountains (including myself) or to rural areas during the Covid pandemic. And stayed. Working remotely and enjoying outdoor activities almost every day is the biggest dream fulfilled and can never be measured in money.

When we do go off on longer vacation, it's absolutely crucial that we let the employees enjoy their time off without interruptions. Some like to check in here and there, and some to be totally unreachable. Accommodate whatever the need is. The ability to make individual setups with employees is what makes a great leader. Don't demand conformity. Don't demand anything. Support instead.

COMMUNICATION

The art of letting others in the organisation now what's going on and making them be able to access the information when they need it, if they need it.

CHAPTER 36

COMMUNICATING

Sharing your company communication over Slack isn't really that uncommon.

In this remote working world — where many teams are spread out doing "home office", we really need to communicate harder, better and smarter. I'm no communication expert, but in the same concept as the other chapters I'm sharing some of my findings of what's good to do and not to do. Communication can be very helpful, and can go very wrong.

The thinking goes that in a traditional office environment (well, ":ish") — there would be gatherings and announcements made, and people would receive the message and be able to ask questions back. That's not really true. Best case there is a "town hall" where you need to be a very strong person to dare to talk in front of everyone, if you'd manage to even get the microphone when you held up your arm. Also, I dare you to say anything negative in front of all your managers and salary payers. Didn't think so.

So what really happens is that people talk in small little groups. Back when people were smoking, some were talking in their little smoke group. People used Skype and nowadays Slack and Teams etc. They talk and chat and write and express themselves all the time. Ever gone in to a room full of developers? (Back when people used to work in offices). Every single one would have earphones on and would rather be writing to each other than to break someones music listening flow by interrupting with something as weird as something spoken. I once witnessed an entire 15-people dev team sit entirely still and clatter away on their keyboard, just to unison-ally stand up at exactly the same time. Why? A Slack message to go for lunch.

It's no secret to CTO's that devs like their chats. Ok – you can also build in cool code integrations and get notifications and whatnot in Slack, but that's beside the point. Most developers I've met rather write a long text than "Walk and talk".

■■

This behaviour takes us to the obvious topic of company communication, Slack/Chat usage and team work. In my semi-humble opinion, I think that all "official" communication should happen via Slack. It's easy to consume and can be sticky if it's in channels for this purpose. It also invites comments and discussions — just like communication should be. Of course — conflicts, people issues, hiring & firing and 1:1 meetings, I think should at least be over video. It can easily be misunderstood and it's better to communicate with our entire body expression than just what we can fire off from our finger tips. Company communication shouldn't also be too adjusted and spun — it'll only alienate people. If things are not clear or not spoken, people will guess. So better be direct. It's a good idea if the communication goes to the people who has an interest in reading it. Meaning - the people affected.

Having access to Slack and the instant replies, could also mean we get too much information, and we never have the chance to work and finish stuff because of the constant notifications. Here we all need to manage our own notifications, but also turn them off for a while if we need to concentrate on something. Don't demand your developers are always online. We do not need to be available all the time. Also not everything needs to be shared and discussed.

Keeping communication to the right level engages and motivates. It's also important that people consumes the info they themselves feel they need, or seek it. If we get a "I wasn't informed about that" — it's a sign of low accountability but could also mean that we failed in letting the right people know.

CHAPTER 37

PROJECT UPDATES

How to communicate what's being worked on, what's going to be worked on and what's done.

People either directly involved in your project or product or affected by the outcome of your activities will need to be continuously getting status updates throughout the process.

You have the great Kanban board and as the leader you know very well what's being worked on – you just check the In Progress column. But others in the organisation may find this information overwhelming. It's a good idea to think thru how you want to communicate updates to others in the organisation. It's also better to be proactive than to wait for others to ask. You'll get a higher buy-in, more participation and people will get more excited. And with you working in an agile style – you can deliver many things often in small iterations.

There's also the other side of this. If you or someone in your team is not responsible for communication – there's a risk that people will go directly to ask the developers. You don't want to put them in a situation where they either have to respond to questions like "when is it done" or "why isn't it done yet” or even worse the “I want it do be done now”. This goes against all principles of a predictable continuous development flow. Don’t get me wrong. If the team is cross-functional they can communicate between themselves as much as they want. What I mean is the micro managers sneaking in.

Holding bi-weekly meetings you could invite the people who wants to get updates on a more detailed level where you can also answer questions or concerns.

For everyone else in the organisation, it may be easier if they join a Slack channel that you setup, where updates are posted.

Going for more than three week time gaps between updates may decrease the trust and engagement in your project from your colleagues or higher management. Short, simple and focused update meetings are always appreciated.

CHAPTER 38

BUDGET

How a stable budget work helps you be geared to run a great team.

Owning your own budget could really help you and your team to be able to work efficiently and to the point. The beauty of budgets is that they are decided once per year (and probably negotiated in the end of the year) and the...er...not so nice part is that they will most likely be tried to be cut by your hostile and non-IT affluent CFO that you happen to report to for some weird organisational reason. To get rid of a lot of issues, including having to explain why your servers needs more CPU (processing power) or disk space to the aforementioned Chief Money Saver, demand to get your own budget. Easy as that. Then you only have to negotiate *once* (hopefully) per year. A nice thing about working with Kanban and Agile development processes is that the cost is predictable. Projects always come with great surprises and has never delivered "on time and on scope" (and within cost). This is the classic triple constrain. If you fix cost and time (12 months...), you can fiddle around with scope. What I'm saying here is that with fixed costs for developers, either as employees, dedicated teams (consultants) our completely outsourced, you can fix the costs. Making a budget based on predictable monthly costs will make budgeting and the accruals work easy. Following up, approving invoices is a no-brainer if you know what's going to come. Most cloud services has monthly subscriptions (unless you divide the yearly in 12) and it will be easy for you and the person approving your budget, what things will cost through the year. With a predictable cost structure, you can also predict the development speed. I say predict, as estimate is not really correct. After a while you know what your team is able to achieve and you don't need to spend your time on too many fancy KPI's or try to "control" the output.

Keep your budget high level. Budget in 1000s and the numbers will look smaller and easier to follow. This is not a trick, it's standard. Pad and add some margins for salary increases, extra server space and other things you think could be a topic over the year.

■■

Armed with your budget you now have the major decisions already taken! Away with the days when you had to get certain time spend on new features approved or you listed your projects to try to be able to justify hours spent on certain activities with a non IT-person. With this component removed, it's up to you how to deliver on the Road Map and business priority.

CHAPTER 39

KPI'S AND OKR'S

Don't measure what you can't control.

Once upon a time when I worked as an Engineering Manager I was asked by the CEO to report on certain KPI's in order to measure and control performance of the development team. We had KPI's (Key Performance Indicators) such as "Development hours per developer and day" measured by that the developers reported time spent every day. Jira's per developer, hours worked on technical tickets, percentage of working days spent in meetings, Average time in X status, etc, etc. The list goes on and on. I even appraised the team with the most working hours per week. Gave budget for team dinners. I was so wrong. If I would be asked the same today, I would not do it that way. Let me be clear, time spent on developing something has **nothing** to do with performance or output or anything. What it does though, is that it tries to measure something in order for it to be controlled. This is from the old factory notion that: "What you don't measure you can't control" which was also popular in old school waterfall project management. What it does do is taking your attention away from what's important, the people. Trying to convert their efforts to numbers. It's not possible, and will be wrong. Also as a KPI. The reasons for development teams to be able to deliver great code is culture, motivation and flow – let them do their thing. Don't interrupt with a lot of nonsense.

KPI's are used to set certain standards and to be able to compare with others. If you are down, it indicates manufacturing is going slower than predicted, or what the competitors are making. This leads to a higher cost per unit and profitability will be less. KPI's was and are still widely used to measure progress and see if a certain activity is performing as planned and expected.

Whit that said, some interesting companies has worked with OKRs (Objective and Key Results). While KPI's are measured against targets, OKRs is an objective tied to a key result. OKRs are ambitious, quantifiable, can be objectively scored and time-lined. This was used by some innovative organisations that usually comes up as good examples: Google, Spotify, Amazon and LinkedIn. OKR's was designed to be able to try to achieve higher goals which was almost impossible. They have this structure:

Objective: Build the best app

> **Key Result #1:** Get $10M in Revenue
>
> **Key Result #2:** Get 25% more bookings
>
> **Key Result #3:** Increase new customers by 20%

■■

I personally think OKR's are superior to KPI's as they are more high level but still measurable. It's also much more clear than to look at "Sales per employee" or "Ticket resolution time". And if you are working in a larger organisation it's a good idea to have a unified way you want to go together.

When it comes to development and developers, the closest I have come to a good KPI to use is "Life Cycle Time" which can be a way to see on average how long time it takes for a ticket/story to go from idea to production — but also here it can depend on so many other outside factors.

It's better to look at outcomes instead of outputs. Meaning – how did it work? Did your users (customers) actually use it, and did it increase the usage of your application? Did you get the feedback you aimed for? Just shooting out features and not look at the outcome is a bit of waste I'd say. This is the data that you want — the adoption data. Act on it. One of the Agile principles says "*Working software is the primary measure of progress.*" That is really true here. Working software means someone is using it and it works.

Another great KPI is how long time it takes to setup a developers local environment. If that takes a week, you may have other issues. The best I have seen is a 1-3 hours. The worst – two weeks. And no one knew anything.

So to end off — measure your success by looking at the outcome. Is it used? Does it work? Lot's of complaints? What's the feedback? This is the most valuable KPI.

CHAPTER 40

BOARD PRESENTATIONS

A story is better than a thousand KPI's.

As with all other chapters, I start with a slight existential question. Are you regularly invited to report to the board? Some organisations still think that their CTO's are IT managers, or a scaled up Developer who can "fix the website". If you find yourself in any of those organisations, I would strongly advice you to pack your bag and leave, or stay and seek more experience on *how to not do it*. A CTO is a C-level title. Yep, sure, many startups uses the C-title and we can spend another chapter on discussing the in's and out's of what a CTO is and is not. In some cases the CTO is reporting to the CFO (very bad idea, how can you leverage innovation by looking at cost controlling only?) or the CEO - which takes it on themselves to "carry the word from the IT-manager" to the board. So much things gets lost in translation. We can agree that most companies has a board and that there are board meetings held, and if the board is discussing future strategy as they maybe should, from my point of view the CTO should have an invitation. Not only because so many decisions are taken by people who have no clue about technology and how it works, more than their own experience and what others have told them. It's a very good idea to have someone who can actually realise things and make it happen. But the single most important reason is that Technology is the core of if not all but most companies today. So if you have a CTO, get them in that meeting. If you are the CTO, get in to that meeting. If not, your hands will be tied and you'd have to sway to the notions of the CEO. We have all been there.

Right, so we are in the meeting. What do we do here? We lead innovation. It can be the classic updates about how special projects are going, sure – but I'd rather focus on bringing to attention the many creative ideas that has come from the team and needs the boards attention that it could be a great thing to test to do. I bet you'll also be reporting on some KPIs but as we concluded in that chapter, they are just indicators of effort and doesn't really support innovation.

■■

Telling the story from a technical and product perspective it's what's really interesting. So you did try the MVP approach for a new feature, you got the feedback by looking at the clicks and actions of the users, and then you went in to another iteration and built a better version which also was adopted well by the users. Great! This is what the board members wants to hear. Remember, they are in their positions because of their experience and long business life. They are probably in other boards too. A story is what is interesting.

The same goes if you had not so successful MVP approach ideas — tell the story. Never ever hide anything from the board, or try to cover it up by blaming others. As a CTO it's ultimately your responsibility to drive innovation and support your teams to make it happen. A story about something that didn't work is also a very good lesson learned for the board.

How you tell the story is up to you — but no one wants "death by Powerpoint" so I'd rather show a timeline with high level historical events to support your story. No need to dive in to details, it's the helicopter perspective that's interesting here.

A part from you and your story, you will grow a relation with the board members and you all need that, as you can and will learn a lot from these experts, so be open to new angles and other experiences. Be their best advisor and offer solutions and innovation.

CHAPTER 41

SOCIAL MEDIA

Online presence – what to write and what to share.

As the CTO, or any other person with a separate title responsible for tech teams, you are a spokes person for the company in a way, and what you share and do on social media like LinkedIn is going to be associated with the company whether you like it or not. This doesn't mean I think you should hold back and not post or comment, but maybe think another second before pressing "Send". Getting in to trolling-comment feeds with endless discussions is also maybe not very productive. You can also turn this little space of yours in to something interesting. Remember that most people who sees what you are posting and commenting are people in your current network. Your employees, co-workers, team members.

Hence, writing posts about topics of your concern is a great way to get to know you and what you stand for. As long as you are an open and approachable leader. Some maybe is better to write in the internal Slack. And we all know what we think of posts like "Look how awesome I am because I took a selfie with a person in a vulnerable position." So spare me that.

■■

If your company are indeed in the forefront of awesome things like letting your co-workers work from anywhere (Way to go Airbnb!) or that you pay out 6 months extra maternity (and paternity) leave — why not publish those stories to the world? It will help your brand. If it's true. One thing that's so nice with Social Media, is that we do have Glassdoor and other employer rating services which shows "the truth", what's usually not learned during the job interview. I would avoid asking all employees to leave a "great review". It shouldn't work like that, but it does work like that. Recommending each other on LinkedIn though, works like that. You have to ask each other in order to get it.

Social media is a great way to read interesting topics and learn more about the **experience of others**. Which is always interesting. Many does have an agenda, but it's their own agenda (mostly, unless they are from troll farms) and that's fine. Pick and choose what makes sense to you.

Me personally still think it's brilliant. Almost everything I've done has come thru LinkedIn in some way. Either it was a new job opportunity, I got to hire new great people, read some insightful article, got new contacts or laughed at that developer joke. So thanks!

CHAPTER 42

FORBIDDEN WORDS LIST

Throw out the old ways, in with the new. Let's stop comparing those apples and oranges.

A common language is what keeps us understanding each other. So when we speak about certain business terms, we may use words for one thing even though we may mean another. And, sometimes a word has a strong meaning for someone, while for you it's just a few letters.

When it comes to working more agile and respond to changes — many of the old school business words are not useful anymore, as they imply things that no longer exists. So here is the list!

■■

Forbidden word	**means**	**Say instead**	**means**
Milestone	A time based end or middle station for a project	Achievement	A place where we can be proud of some outcome
Deadline	Newspaper is print over night so you better release before this	Release estimate	Estimated release but depending on other factors that can occur
Asap	Do this now because I need it now	Raise priority	Move it higher up the list as it's important
Task	Something that needs to be done	Story	Someone is doing something and this is what happens, maybe this should happen instead
Deliverable	A package of features for a release	Feature	A single feature that can be released separately and without dependencies
Project	A package of activities that has a start and an end	Product	An ever improving Product which is never ever done

Resource	Person who works in a project	Co-worker	A real human being who has feelings, motivations, ideas, makes assumptions and is not perfect
Working hours	The amount of time someone spend at the computer	Outcome	The actual result of the entire idea when it's released to production and is generating feedback
Critical path	The chain of activities that must not be disturbed as if it is then everything else will take longer time	Iteration	An improvement to the product, released as a small, non-dependent complete solution (can vertically cover all parts)

Meeting	A never ending babble of uninteresting things and a repeat of what everyone already knows	Standup	A time boxed quick information sharing about "What I did since yesterday", "What I will do until tomorrow" and "This is the issue I have"
Update	A micro managers check up from employees on how far they have come on the task what was given	See Standup	
Demo	A demonstration of the product to the big important stakeholder where everyone is nervous	Show off	A fun and exciting time when developers show off their cool stuff that they are proud of

Quality Assurance	A rigorous testing procedure which has the ultimate goal to make sure the high quality of a software is held by imposing a battery of testing by people who was not involved coding it	Test	A nice mix of the developers own responsibility to test what they built themselves, some test code, some automated tests and some help from the reporters or the Product Owner to see that it makes sense.
Failure	Something that was not good at all and should always be avoided	Learning	Something that was not good, but got fixed and it was learned and appreciated
Over-budget	Something costs way more than what the first specification said it would	Improved	Something that added a lot of value by improving the features as it went and left a much better product than what was ever possible to think up before

Gold plated	Adding extra time and effort to change something that was not agreed to in the contract before	Improvement	Building a feature better by allowing some minor changes that you could only learn when you looked at it
Late	The deadline which was written in the project charter 7 months ago and communicated in the Steering Committee has been passed.	De-prioritised	Other things came up which was more important and by focusing on them the product is a much better one.
Scope	The range of functions that the product should do and only those.	Backlog	A list of stories that are prioritised according to the business need and is an honest and transparent view of what needs to be done.

Phase	One of the clearly separated activity groups of the project which has the aim to go to another phase (ie Planning, Execution, Testing, Release)	See Iteration	
Cycle	A cycle of activities happening within a Phase (Scrum-fall)	See Iteration	
Approved	A manager with a higher salary and thus more self-perceived importance needs to say yes and micro manage it before it can be released	Peer reviewed	A co-worker who gives their feedback and suggests changes before it *is* released
Request	An order from a superior ranking manager to perform a task	Suggestion	A friendly feedback or idea of an improvement that can be passed on to the responsible team

Highest priority		Focus area	
Office	A centrally located building where all employees had to commute to and stay in for their entire working day. Mostly so it was checked so people actually worked. Popular between 1950 to 2020.	Meeting and in person collaborating space	A place that can be rented or used on request when people need to meet in person to be creative and collaborate.
Policy	A set of rules decided by the top management that must be followed.	Basic commitments	A set of jointly agreed statements that is agreed to be the co-workers themselves.

Working time	The amount of clock time an employee spends working by the computer. Usually set to 8 per day, excluding or including short breaks.	Availability	A time span within an employee is working and thus is available to do work, which they are doing independently. It does not mean you can always call or invite to meetings. It doesn't mean they are sitting by the computer.
End User	The ultimate user, using your software.	Customer/ Guest	The most important guest getting a thought thru experience clicking thru your application.
Manager	Someone who controls and directs work.	Leader	Someone who leads by example and delegates to autonomous teams. A coach and a facilitator.

Ensure	Must make sure it is done in a way so that the manager who said the word doesn't look bad in front of their superiors again.	Make possible	A way to improve working ways and processes to make it possible that negative outcomes are minimised.
Fix it	Just do whatever it takes to make it work without telling the manager how it was done so that they can say to superiors that it's done.	Facilitate change	Actively engage co-workers and find ways to solve issues and prevent negative outcomes.
Vacation/Time off	An employees time not working.	Breathe space	A way for the co-worker to take a step away from work and actually live.
Lunch break	A time boxed slot where the employee can stuff their face with food.	Recharger	An unavailable blocked time when the co-worker can engage in activities such as eating food, exercising or just rest.

Employees	People on a payroll that gets their wage from the company.	Co-workers	Valued peers who are engaged, contributes and are committed.
HR - Human Resources	The practice of trying to make top managements decision on salaries, work conditions and recruitment to meet with laws and at the same time keep employees employed so someone can do the work.	People-people	An active partner to *both* leaders and co-workers who can help and facilitate discussions and implement human and caring ways on how to collaborate and be around each other.
Agenda	The before decided list of things to discuss on the meeting.	Focus points	The main topics of discussion, giving also space for other things to be discussed if needed.
Top-down	Order from the far away management team, that may or may not be based on reality.	Micro managed	Telling a work group or team how they should do a certain thing (not the what) is micro management.

Bottom-up	The notion that the employees are in the bottom, the lowest rank, and they come up with an idea that gets implemented in the organisation	Self organised	The autonomous self-organised and self-managed team that comes up with ideas and implements them as they see fit themselves.
Project Manager	The person who plans, gather information and formally leads the Project and informs Stakeholders about the progress.	Facilitator	A person who facilitates activities and make them happen by engaging and leading people.
Scrum Master	A name of the person facilitating the scrum process in an agile scrum project.	See Facilitator	
Status update	A meeting to check how far people have come on the tasks they have been given.	Standup meeting	A meeting for the co-workers to share their progress with peers and ask for help if they are stuck.

Kickoff	A company wide meeting to start a new season or sales period.	Powerpoint day	What it really is. Bring popcorn.
Offsite	A company meeting outside the office for some joint activities and to bond.	Activity day	Now that most people are working remotely, the day is not an offsite anymore and can instead be an activity day, perhaps even done in multiple locations at the same time.
Idiot	The employee who didn't deliver and wasn't doing their job.	Not in the right place / given the right conditions	The co-worker who was placed in the wrong setting without the prerequisites needed and was not able to contribute.

Vendor	An external company delivering services or products.	Collaboration Partner	A partner which one can involve and have an integrated part of the entire Product development. A partner who shares success and learnings.
External consultant	Someone from another company that's just here to do a specific job and not worth spending any time with. Classic us and them.	Co-worker	Really just another co-worker who needs interaction, discussions and feedback as anyone else.
Team lead	A person responsible for the delivery of a team.	Chief Enabler	A real leader who supports and facilitates the process.
Annual review	The yearly goal go thru and feedback session.	Feedback to company	The chance for the company to get feedback from their co-workers instead.

Rollout	A multi-channel/stream release to production with high risk and hard to revert.	Test release	A release of a small (vertical) part of the feature(s) that moves the product to the next incremental rather than a big bang. See Iteration.
Handover	The formal process of handing over work to another team or employee.	Product Development	The same team who built it maintains and improves it.

THE END

Thanks for reading my book.

Writing this book was fun, challenging and a learning process. I had to look at my work life in the review mirror and perform a true retrospective. When I was trying to find business examples I had to review how we worked in different companies. It's interesting to see that there are so many ways of working. Nothing is really correct and many things are similar, it just has a different name.

Writing a book may be seen a major achievement, but it's really just to brain dump down all thoughts and try to organise them. Or as my friend Jacob said, "Agile book release". And that's what I've been doing. In true iterative Agile style I have been releasing small improvements, either based on feedback or just weird formulations I found proof reading another round.

Big thanks to Jacob Midtgaard-Olesen (ex CTO of Umbraco, now CTO and Co-Founder of Recoverlution) for the many insights and your mentorship. Let's take the hobbits to Isengard!

ABOUT THE AUTHOR

At the time of writing this book I'm working as a CTO-consultant helping companies to realise their tech products — leading development teams and driving Agile change. Are you interested in getting in touch with me?

Robert Mejlerö
robert@mejlero.com
https://www.linkedin.com/in/robertmejlero/

+41 78 982 17 62
The Mejlerö Company GmbH
https://mejlero.com

Printed in Great Britain
by Amazon